Sacajawea

UNIVERSITY OF OKLAHOMA PRESS : NORMAN

Sacajawea

HAROLD P. HOWARD

International Standard Book Number: 0–8061–0967–X
Library of Congress Catalog Card Number: 70–160495

Copyright 1971 by the University of Oklahoma Press, Publishing Division of the University. Composed and printed at Norman, Oklahoma, U.S.A., by the University of Oklahoma Press. First edition.

Preface

FEW personalities in American history have been more idealized—or more controversial—than Sacajawea, the Shoshoni Indian girl who accompanied Meriwether Lewis and William Clark on their expedition to the Pacific Coast in 1804–1806. Some historians, among them Samuel Eliot Morison and LeRoy R. Hafen, refer to her as a guide or interpreter for the party. Others call her an unofficial "ambassadress" to the Indians living in the regions through which the explorers passed. Her importance to the expedition has also been disputed. Early twentieth-century historians tended to glorify her role. More recent writers are inclined to minimize her contribution and even to adopt a somewhat scornful view of her assistance to the explorers. It is the purpose of this book to review what has been learned and conjectured about her life before, during, and after the expedition and to accord to this appealing woman her rightful place in the westward expansion of the United States.

Sacajawea's life, like that of other native Americans who played brief but important roles on the stage of American history, must be largely pieced together from contemporary accounts—from the journals, diaries, and notes of Lewis and Clark and other members of the expedition. From those records it seems clear that Sacajawea joined the expedition largely by accident. She was allowed to accompany her French-Canadian husband, Toussaint Charbonneau, who was hired in the Mandan villages in South Dakota to serve as an interpreter on the journey westward. Sacajawea was one of the two unofficial members of the party, the other being Clark's black servant, York. Moreover, she was an unlikely member: she carried a newborn son. Yet it may be that her greatest service, among the many she performed, was simply her presence among the hardy band of explorers. The Indians the expedition encountered along the way knew that a woman with a baby never accompanied a war party. Her presence assured them that the explorers' intentions were peaceful.

After the Lewis and Clark party returned to South

Dakota, Sacajawea's service to the expedition ended. For many years afterward her name was almost lost to history. Contemporary records indicate that she died in her twenties in South Dakota. Indian tradition gives her a long life, the latter part spent in Wyoming with her people.

Contemporary records make it fairly easy to trace the later life of Sacajawea's husband, Charbonneau. Sacajawea's subsequent life is much more difficult to ascertain. Over the years the mists of legend tended to obscure the real woman. All that is known today about her and her family can be found in the pages that follow, with due attention to what many accept as authentic Indian oral tradition.

Americans are sentimental about their heroines. More memorials honor Sacajawea than any other American woman. Monuments, markers, and shafts have been erected in her honor, and parks, lakes, and mountain peaks have been named for her. This book, the product of many years spent in research and in sifting fact from romance, represents an effort at an unbiased appraisal of Sacajawea and her achievements.

To make clear Sacajawea's contribution to the success of the Lewis and Clark Expedition, I have found it necessary to retrace the path of the expedition in some detail, relating events in which Sacajawea took no direct or recorded part. Her daily assistance to the explorers—primarily as a provider of edible wild food—was often accepted without comment. Only in moments of crisis or times of deprivation was her aid acknowledged. Yet the explorers were aware of and grateful for her presence—as I hope to make clear in the pages that follow.

I wish to express thanks to many persons who have helped

Sacajawea

in the preparation of this book by offering useful advice and criticism—especially Ardis Edwards Burton, of Crockett, California; T. A. Larson, of the University of Wyoming; and Will G. Robinson, former secretary of the South Dakota Historical Society.

HAROLD P. HOWARD

Stickney, South Dakota
March 15, 1971

Contents

Illustrations

Maps

PART ONE: *The Lewis and Clark Expedition*

The Expedition Sets Out

THE Lewis and Clark Expedition was a favorite project of President Thomas Jefferson. He had dreamed of this journey of exploration long before 1803, when his emissaries managed to buy the Louisiana Territory from Napoleon I of France for fifteen million dollars.

Before he received congressional approval of the Louisiana Purchase, and almost before the ink was dry on the document of sale, Jefferson set in motion his plan to explore the vast wilderness northwest of the Mississippi River. The land included in the Louisiana Purchase extended to the western border of what is now Montana. He expected the explorers to go beyond the limits of the newly acquired territory, and he hoped that they would find a traversable land or land-and-river route to the Pacific Ocean.

Jefferson had already decided who would lead this proposed expedition—Captain Meriwether Lewis, whom Jefferson first employed as his secretary, probably in anticipation of the expedition. Captain Lewis in turn had already decided whom he wanted to share the command if he could be persuaded to go—Captain William Clark, the younger brother of the famed Revolutionary War general George Rogers Clark. Lewis wrote to Clark from Washington on June 19, 1803, and received a favorable reply from Kentucky on July 26. Lewis insisted upon joint command of the expedition, wanting Clark to have authority equal to his own and to share equally in all decisions.

The expedition assembled in the fall of 1803 near St. Louis, Missouri, a village then consisting of just three streets. To begin with, the party numbered, besides the two captains, nine young Kentucky volunteers; fourteen soldiers, also volunteers; two French rivermen; one hunter; and Clark's Negro servant, York. To accompany them by water as far as the Mandan Indian villages in what is now North Dakota, nine more boatmen were employed, along with seven more soldiers. Winter quarters were established at Wood River on the eastern side of the Mississippi, opposite the mouth of the Missouri.

Jefferson's instructions said: "The object of your mission

is to explore the Missouri River, & such principal streams of it, as by its course & communication with the waters of the Pacific Ocean, may offer the most direct and practicable water communication across this continent, for the purpose of commerce." Lewis and Clark were expected to learn about the Indians, draw maps, find specimens of everything new to them—minerals, trees, flowers, animals, birds—and keep journals. Their cataloguing of these discoveries, and much more, is incredibly detailed. For the journey the explorers received altogether a niggardly appropriation of twenty-five-hundred dollars from Congress. Fortunately, they were able to draw on army depots for additional supplies.[1]

The materials most necessary for the expedition were divided into bales and boxes, one box containing a little of everything in the case of accidents. The men packed clothing, fine instruments, tools, locks, flints, powder, ammunition, medicines, and articles of a critical nature in seven bales and one reserve box. To these were added fourteen bales and one box of Indian presents—fancy coats, medals, flags, knives, tomahawks, ornaments, looking glasses, handkerchiefs, paints, and beads. The heaviest single item was lead for bullets. Spirits and tobacco were also included.

The party pulled away from the Wood River base on May 14, 1804, and proceeded up the Missouri River past a few small settlements. Very infrequently were they entirely

---

[1] The expedition finally cost more than $38,000, including army pay, subsistence, bounties, clothing, special uniforms, disbursements for horses, and so on, as well as the cost of outfitting and conducting a party of Mandan Indians to Washington in 1806 and returning them to Mandan country.

waterborne, since some members of the party usually walked along the shore. The plan was to go up the Missouri to its headwaters, which were thought to be several thousand miles away, and then strike off across the mountains, if necessary, to find a river leading to the Pacific Ocean.

For this water journey the men had procured a fifty-five-foot keelboat with a small sail and twenty-two oars. The men added two boats called pirogues, forty to fifty feet long, twelve feet wide, pointed at the prow, and square-sterned. Two horses, for hunting or carrying meat, were led or ridden along the banks of the river. The party pulled, poled, rowed, or sailed the boats up the river, always against the current.

The difference between this expedition and earlier and subsequent efforts to make the transcontinental journey was that the Lewis and Clark Expedition was well equipped and well planned. At times it would seem that there was too much baggage and that too much time was spent taking notes. But the result of the expedition was the opening of a land-and-river route across the United States—not the best or the shortest, but a good one—and the accumulation of a wealth of scientific information. The captains also drew the first good maps of the region.

A comparison of the Lewis and Clark trip, which was made into a completely unknown area, with the Astorians' trip of 1811, seven years later, points up how well Lewis and Clark managed. The Astorians tried to make the trip partly by water and partly by land, and they nearly failed to reach their destination, although Lewis and Clark had opened the way.

Another reason for the success of the Lewis and Clark Expedition was the alertness of the leaders. They always posted guards, and they seemed to be able to anticipate trouble. Lewis brought along his big Newfoundland, Scannon, who proved useful as a watchdog and hunter. Most of the Indian tribes ate dog meat, and Lewis and Clark did too; at times they even considered it a delicacy. But because of his value to the expedition Scannon never became a stew, and once a search party was sent out to find him when he was stolen by Indians.

Sir Alexander Mackenzie, an intrepid Scottish explorer, had reached the Pacific Ocean through the Canadian Rockies about a dozen years before the Americans arrived there. Responsible for only a boatload of men, Mackenzie followed such a mountainous route that it could not be developed. Although he moved 17,500 miles up and down Canadian rivers and another 500 miles on foot, he collected little scientific information, and by comparison with Lewis and Clark's journals his reports make dull reading.

Mackenzie's home base was at Lake Athabasca, near the Canadian Rockies, to which he could repair when he went in the wrong direction in his search for the Pacific Ocean. Mackenzie went northwest in 1789, all the way up the river that now bears his name and to the Arctic Ocean. In 1792 he explored the Peace River and found a short portage route across the mountains, reaching the Pacific above Vancouver Island, but no highway follows that route today.

Lewis and Clark were expected to succeed the first time, and the key to their success was skillful preparation. To begin with, they made few mistakes in calculating the amount of supplies necessary. One of their misjudgments was to carry too few blue beads, which the far-western Indian tribes cherished. Another was to haul halfway across the continent an iron framework for a boat, which Lewis planned to cover with skins or bark. The idea was a failure. Otherwise, the leaders' logistics were infallible. One of their most important precautions was to take along a full assortment of gun parts, even though they started with new guns. They lost some supplies, but accidents could not be foreseen or avoided.

In preparing for the rest of their journey, the captains made several fortunate decisions after they reached the Mandan villages, thereby proving they were good geographers who made no serious errors in their route.

The journey did not become a true exploration until the explorers reached the Mandans. All of the lower part of the Missouri River had been traveled by traders. The explorers passed through regions (later to be part of ten states of the United States), starting by crossing what is now the state of Missouri. From the west edge of the Missouri, the river flows from the north between Missouri and Iowa, between Missouri and Nebraska for a short stretch, and between Iowa and Nebraska. At the southeastern tip of South Dakota the river angles northwest into North Dakota, and near present-day Bismarck it passes through what was then the land of the Mandans and the Hidatsas.

The diaries kept by members of the expedition call attention to storms, heat, sandbars, snags, and treacherous currents, but in the early stages of their journey (across present-day Missouri, Iowa, Nebraska, and Kansas) they also remark on the beauty and richness of the countryside beyond the Missouri River bluffs.

The adventurers met few Indians and fewer white traders on their laborious trip upriver. To the Indians they gave variations of their "Great White Father" speech, urging them to discard Spanish and French medals and flags and to accept American medals and flags. Before they reached the Mandans, lack of an interpreter handicapped them.

There were some lapses of discipline. The "Corps of Discovery" was not yet a tightly integrated group.[2] In each instance the captains court-martialed the offending men and flogged them when necessary. Before long the men were under military control. There was one death, early in the journey, the only death throughout the course of the expedition. Sergeant Charles Floyd, of Kentucky, died on August 20, 1804, near present-day Sioux City, Iowa, probably from a ruptured appendix and peritonitis. The captains named a river for him, and today a monument to him stands in the vicinity.

The first crisis that threatened the progress of the expedition began on September 25 and continued for three days. A series of confrontations took place with the warlike Teton Sioux in what is now south-central South Dakota. The captains slept little during this crisis. Trouble was expected with the Indians, and the men were prepared for it, for the Sioux had stopped earlier trading parties and had forced them to dispose of their goods for little or nothing.

On September 25, Lewis and Clark faced the Sioux, turning swivel guns on them. The following three days were mostly anticlimactic, and from that time on the Tetons did not molest them.

On October 27 the expedition reached the Five Villages

2 The Corps of Discovery was a title probably suggested by Captain Lewis. Lewis signed his papers as "Captain, 1st Infantry" and Clark as "Captain of Corps of Discovery."

of the Mandans in North Dakota. In the 1730's the Mandans had lived in the region around present-day Bismarck. It was there that white men first encountered them. They later retreated upriver about sixty miles to avoid the Sioux. Lewis and Clark found them near the mouth of the Knife River. Besides a village of Mandans there were two villages of Hidatsas and a settlement of relatives of the latter, whom the journals refer to as "Wettersoons." These Indians had substantial, livable dwellings, lodges made of timber, sunk partly into the ground and covered with thick roofs of earth. Most important, they were friendly.

The Journals and Diaries

2

IN accordance with President Jefferson's instructions, everyone on the Lewis and Clark Expedition was urged to keep a diary. Besides the two captains, apparently three of the twenty-three privates and four sergeants did so. The members of the party had been selected for their ability to withstand the rigors of life on the trail, rather than for their writing ability. Sometimes it was more important to kill

11

game or find one's way back to camp than to compose a
narrative or keep a diary. It must have been a great effort
not only to write by firelight at the end of a difficult day's
travel but also to protect notes from the elements.

The journal that Captain Clark kept is more nearly com-
plete than that of Captain Lewis. It contains a daily record
for all but ten days of the entire journey (a single entry
covers those ten days). The records of 441 days of the expedition are missing from Lewis' journal. Often the two
captains' records parallel each other, occasionally making it
appear that one of the men copied from the other's log—
borrowing perhaps made necessary by accident or illness.

Privates Joseph Whitehouse, Robert Frazier (or Frazer),
and George Shannon recorded some of their experiences.
Whitehouse's writings cover the period from May 14, 1804,
to November 6, 1805. His journal was given to someone who
later sold it to a private collector in 1894. Reuben Gold
Thwaites, the famed Wisconsin historian, found and purchased the Whitehouse journal in the early 1900's. Frazier's
diary was lost, and only a few of his maps were found.

The journal of one of the four sergeants, Nathaniel Pryor,
was also lost. Sergeant Charles Floyd kept a faithful record
until his death on August 20, 1804, mentioned earlier. His
journal, lost for eighty-five years, was found by Thwaites in
1895. Patrick Gass, who was elected sergeant after Floyd's
death and who had attended school only fourteen days in
his life, kept a journal that was edited and embellished by a
schoolmaster and published in 1807. It gives a great deal of
useful information about the expedition.[1]

[1] Gass gave his book a splendid title: *A Journal of the Voyages and
Travels of a Corps of Discovery Under the Command of Captain*

The journal of Sergeant John Ordway, for many years believed lost, was also found by Thwaites. Parts of it were owned by the heirs of Captain Clark, and other parts eventually became part of the Nicholas Biddle estate. Biddle, a prominent Philadelphia lawyer, publisher, and diplomat, edited the notes for the first official narrative of Lewis and Clark's travels, having been persuaded to do so by Captain Clark. Biddle's work was completed by Paul Allen, a writer whom he asked to assist him. George Shannon, one of the privates who kept a diary, was employed to help Biddle and Allen interpret the notes. Biddle was a well-educated scholar, and he was thorough. He could write in Latin as well as English, and when he found descriptions of Indian rituals offensive, he put them in Latin in his narrative, although his notes are in English.

Ordway fortunately bridges most of the gaps left by the other diarists. He was one of the better educated of the enlisted men. He guarded his manuscript carefully through the whole arduous journey, keeping it inside his shirt most of the time. Eventually he sold it to Clark for ten dollars.

After the expedition Gass's diary, published in 1810, was the first to be published. Lewis' untimely death in 1809 delayed publication of an "official" account of the expedition, which was finally issued in 1814 in two volumes and became known as the Biddle edition. Two thousand copies

Lewis and Capt. Clark of the Army of the United States, from the Mouth of the River Missouri Through the Interior Parts of North America to the Pacific Ocean, During the years 1804, 1805 and 1806, Containing an Authentic Relation of the Most Interesting Transactions During the Expedition, a Description of the Country and an Account of Its Inhabitants, Soil, Climate and Curiosities and Vegetable and Animal Production.

were to have been printed, but only fourteen hundred copies were actually issued. As far as the records show, Biddle never received any payment for his work.[2]

The Biddle edition was re-edited in 1893 with many notes by Elliott Coues, an army surgeon, naturalist, and surveyor from New Hampshire. Coues retraced many miles of the Lewis and Clark trail, and his geographical notes are of great interest, although he tended to overedit the diaries.

In the years 1904–1906, Thwaites, secretary of the Wisconsin Historical Society, published his eight-volume work on Lewis and Clark, including everything then available on the expedition, in addition to scientific notes and letters, in unabridged form.[3]

[2] Since Biddle was married to a very wealthy woman, payment was probably not important to him.

[3] The quotations in subsequent pages are largely taken from the diaries of Meriwether Lewis or William Clark, and occasionally from the diaries of other members of the expedition. The unedited journals, as published by Thwaites, have a flavor of their own, but they are not easy to read. Spelling is phonetic, punctuation is largely absent, and capitalization follows no rules. Coues re-edited Biddle in 1893, adding a great many useful notes explaining names and locations that would otherwise mean little to the general reader.

Sacajawea Comes to Visit

3

"WE commence building our cabins," Clark wrote on November 3, 1804. The day before he had gone downriver from the Mandan village where they had stopped to look for a suitable campsite with timber nearby. On November 4, Clark mentioned visitors: "A Mr Chaubonie, interpeter for the Gross Ventre nation Came to See us, and informed that [he] came Down with Several Indians from a hunting expedition up the river, to here what we had told the Indians in Council   this man wished to hire as an interpiter."

Thus is introduced Toussaint Charbonneau, Sacajawea's French-Canadian husband. The "Several Indians" referred to by Clark included at least two Indian women. Ordway wrote on the same day: "Frenchman's squaw came to our camp who belongs to the Snake nation. She came with our interpreter's wife and brought with them four buffalo robes and gave them to our officers." The interpreter was a French Canadian named Réné Jussome, a local trader and a friend of Charbonneau's. Jussome was the first interpreter hired by Lewis and Clark, and it is likely that his wife and Sacajawea were the visitors to the camp.[1]

Charbonneau, well known to the Indians of the region,

[1] For one hundred years after the expedition, the Indian girl's name was spelled Sacajawea and pronounced either with both the *Sa* and *we* syllables accented, or with the *ja* syllable accented, as the Shoshonis pronounced it. In time, etymologists decided that the spelling should be Sacagawea or Sakakawea. The phonetic rendering of the name in Hidatsa is Tsi-ki-ka-wi-as, which has apparently become Sakakawea. In Hidatsa the name means Bird Woman. In Shoshoni it means Boat Pusher. The spelling Sacagawea doubtless stems from a reference to her by Clark in his journal. On April 7, 1805, Clark, a phonetic speller, made what appeared to be a special notation in his journal: "Sah-kah-gar-we-a." He may have intended a hard *g* sound in the third syllable. One cannot rely on Clark's spelling, however. In his notes he managed to spell the name Sioux twelve different ways. Ordway, in his diary, makes a reference to Sah-ka-gah. But it appears that Shannon advised Biddle and Allen, who prepared the first official edition of the journals, to spell the name Sacajawea. Shannon was one of the expedition's better spellers and was attending college when he was called upon to assist in editing the journals. In 1893, Elliott Coues, who added many notes to the Biddle edition of the journals, retained the spelling Sacajawea. For historical purposes I have also chosen to use this spelling.

had lived among them for about eight years. Before that he had been with the Northwest Fur Company, and in 1803 he had been at Fort Pembina. The Indians regarded him with some amusement, and through the years they gave him several nicknames, most of them derisive.[2]

Sacajawea must have been a pathetic sight at this time—young (about sixteen years old), small, forlorn. A long way from her home in Idaho, she had been the property of the Hidatsas, who had stolen her from her people, the Shoshonis, and she was now one of Charbonneau's chattels. He had probably acquired her in a gambling game or by barter when she was ten or twelve years old. She was pregnant. Charbonneau had another Shoshoni wife, whose name may have been Otter Woman. He may also have had a Mandan wife; he was constantly marrying Indian girls. It is quite possible that he took both Shoshoni girls as wives at their own request, perhaps because they hoped to stay together. This was marriage *à la façon du pays* ("after the fashion of the country"), as the French said. "Man and wife" simply lived together.

On this occasion the two female visitors to the camp were given some provisions and sent home by the captains. On November 11, Clark noted, "Two Squars of the Rock[y] mountains, purchased from the Indians by a frenchman came down." The younger of the girls on this visit was again Sacajawea.

On November 20 the members of the expedition moved into their winter quarters, which they had named Fort Mandan. They had built two rows of sheds, adjoining at a

[2] Some of the Indian names for Charbonneau were Chief of the Little Village, Great Horse from Afar, and Forest Bear.

right angle. Each row contained four rooms, fourteen feet square and seven feet high, with plank ceilings and slanting roofs. The walls behind the huts were eighteen feet high. Fort Mandan was to be the men's home until April, 1805.

The Indians were interested in the building operations. Clark wrote that three chiefs from one of the Mandan villages stayed all day on November 20. "They are very curious in examining our works."

Winter arrived, and the weather grew increasingly cold. On the morning of December 10 the temperature stood at ten degrees below zero. Nevertheless, the men at the fort tried to preserve the amenities of home. They held a Christmas party, which Sacajawea and other Indian wives attended out of curiosity. On December 25, Gass wrote: "At half past two another gun was fired, as a notice to assemble at the dance, which was continued in a jovial manner till eight at night; and without the presence of any females except three squaws, wives to our interpreter, who took no other part than the amusement of looking on."[3] No other Indians were invited.

Lewis and Clark had employed Jussome, who was familiar with the Mandan tongue, to interpret for them. Charbonneau was employed to accompany the expedition because he could make himself understood by most of the river Indians. He communicated with them chiefly by sign language; he freely admitted that he could not pronounce

---

[3] The favorite musical instruments in the wilderness were the jew's-harp and the harmonica. On this occasion Peter Cruzatte had his violin, and Ordway mentioned "a fiddle, tambereen & a sounden horn," the last probably a bugle or trumpet. The men evidently danced their square dances without women partners.

Indian words correctly. Neither Charbonneau nor Jussome was very highly thought of by the fur traders of the region, who often referred to them as knaves, sneaks, and scoundrels. The captains thought that they could handle Charbonneau, and they were already contemplating Sacajawea's possible usefulness to them later on, if they encountered her tribe.

Lewis and Clark interviewed the Indians who came to their camp out of curiosity or in hope of presents. From their visitors they learned something about the country up-river. They concluded that they would have to portage the Rocky Mountains. Some of the Indians knew about the Great Falls of the Missouri in Montana. Beyond that they were not too informative, but the Hidatsas, who ranged widely, knew that the Shoshoni Indians had horses. It was the Hidatsas who had brought the Shoshoni girls back from present-day southwestern Montana (Sacajawea had been kidnapped by the Hidatsas near the headwaters of the Missouri, at a spot she would later point out to Lewis and Clark).

Some of the Indians were attached to the Fort Mandan garrison during the winter, and the interpreters and their wives were allowed within the stockade. Lewis wrote on February 7: "The sergeant of the guard reported that the Indian women (wives to our interpreters) were in the habit of unbarring the fort gate at any time of night and admitting their Indian visitors." Probably these guests were other women. Lewis directed the men to put a lock on the gate.

One or more of the Indian wives at Fort Mandan may have been present to aid Sacajawea in the delivery of her baby. Lewis and Clark wanted to start up the Missouri as soon as the ice broke up in the spring. They had by now agreed to let Sacajawea accompany Charbonneau, and they hoped that her baby would arrive before the departure. The much anticipated birth occurred on February 11 or 12, 1805. The baby, Sacajawea's first, was a boy. Four diaries, those of Lewis, Ordway, Gass, and Whitehouse, mention his birth. Lewis writes: ". . . her labor was tedious and the pain violent." Although he had brought along a variety of medicines and cures, he was not prepared for childbirth. Everyone made suggestions. Jussome said that he had heard of powdered rattlesnake rattle for difficult births. Wrote Lewis:

Having the rattle of a snake by me, I gave it to [Jussome], and he administered two rings of it to the woman, broken in small pieces with the fingers, and added to a small quantity of water. . . . I was informed that [Sacajawea] had not taken it ten minutes before she brought forth. Perhaps this remedy may be worthy of future experiments, but I must confess that I want faith as to its efficacy.

Ordway did not mention Sacajawea's difficulty in delivery. He wrote only: "An interesting occurrence of this day was the birth of a son of the Shoshone squaw." Gass commented: "On the twelfth we arrived at the fort and found that one of our interpreter's wives had, in our absence, made an addition to our number." The baby was christened Jean Baptiste, later nicknamed "Pomp," Shoshoni for "first-born."

Leaving the Mandans

4

IN the spring of 1805 the Lewis and Clark party, to which
Sacajawea and Charbonneau—and the new baby—had now
been attached, were ready to set out through country almost
completely unknown to white men.

The captains had been able to secure information about
the Missouri River's main tributaries, the first of which was
the Yellowstone (from the south). They had a clear idea of

the distant Great Falls of the Missouri. From the Hidatsa tribe they had learned that there were several possible routes across what came to be known as the Continental Divide, which led to northward-flowing rivers that Lewis and Clark thought might be southern branches of the Columbia River. These routes were described so vaguely to them that the explorers were seldom sure of their actual direction.

The men expected to cross mountains somewhere, and they knew that they would have to acquire some horses. The Shoshonis had horses. The captains concluded that Sacajawea could prove a real asset to the expedition.

By April 7 they were ready to move. Six soldiers and two French hunters were sent downriver to St. Louis in a barge and a canoe to take back papers and reports for President Jefferson and various items the party had collected, among them buffalo robes, Mandan corn, a set of mountain ram horns, a live prairie dog, and four magpies. On the same day the main, or "permanent," party, pushed off upriver for the unknown.

In command was Captain Lewis, a frontiersman of Welsh stock, a moody, introspective young man, thirty years old, a "rambler," as he called himself. He was a lover of nature, a dreamer, and an amateur doctor. He could write a connected narrative, albeit with individualistic spelling and punctuation, for he had had little formal education. He was a serious, dedicated man.

Captain Clark, Lewis' partner in command, was of Scots descent, a frontiersman like Lewis, a good-natured, outgoing man. He was red-headed but notably even-tempered withal. He was thirty-four years old, an experienced geographer, surveyor, and map maker. He expressed himself satisfactorily in writing, though, like Lewis, his spelling was inventive.

These two young captains successfully directed, without serious friction, a group made up of Americans, French Canadians, and Indians—and one Negro, Clark's personal servant, York.

The personnel the two captains led included Sergeants John Ordway, Nathaniel Pryor, and Patrick Gass; Privates William Bratton, John Colter (later to achieve fame as the first white man to discover Jackson Hole, Wyoming[1]), Reuben Fields, Joseph Fields, (brothers), John Shields, George Gibson, George Shannon, John Potts, John Collins, Joseph Whitehouse, Richard Windsor, Alexander Willard, Hugh Hall, Silas Goodrich, Robert Frazier, Peter Cruzatte, Baptiste LePage, Francis Labiche, Hugh McNeal, William Werner, Thomas P. Howard, Peter Wiser, and John B. Thompson. The interpreters were George Drewyer (or Drouillard), Toussaint Charbonneau (at forty-six the oldest member of the expedition), and York (the foregoing names are given variant spellings in the diaries).

A few specialists were included in the party. Gass was an expert carpenter. Drewyer was not only an interpreter but also a skilled hunter. Shields was a gunsmith. Cruzatte was a veteran riverman.

The vessels consisted of six small canoes and two large pirogues, one red and one white. Lewis was pleased to be starting, as he wrote in his diary, and he thought that his little fleet would weather the trip without trouble, although it was "not quite so respectable as that of Columbus or Captain Cook."

[1] See David J. Saylor, *Jackson Hole, Wyoming: In the Shadow of the Tetons,* Norman, 1970.

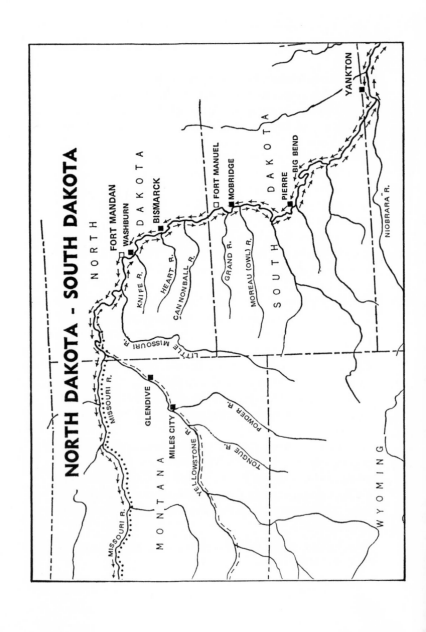

NORTH DAKOTA - SOUTH DAKOTA

NORTH DAKOTA–SOUTH DAKOTA

After spending the first winter on the trail at Fort Mandan, on the Missouri River, the Lewis and Clark Expedition set out in the spring of 1805 for the West.

The Missouri River was the route of the expedition from Wood River, Illinois, north of St. Louis, where the Missouri joins the Mississippi, through all the states since created west of that point, to southwestern Montana, where the explorers left the Missouri and its tributaries to turn west through Lemhi Pass in the Rocky Mountains.

On the return trip from the Pacific Ocean, the party divided. In the summer of 1806, Clark and his men proceeded west from Three Forks, Montana, to the Yellowstone River and followed that river to its junction with the Missouri. Part of Lewis' party went downriver from Great Falls, while another group made a trip up the Marias River, joined the river party at the junction of the Marias with the Missouri, and proceeded down the Missouri for a reunion with Clark and his men.

To orient the reader, present-day state lines and towns have been added to this and subsequent maps.

The men's armament consisted of short rifles made especially for the expedition, pistols, fusils (light flintlock muskets), blunderbusses, a swivel cannon, and an air gun.[2] They also had knives, axes, and spontoons, the last a combination short pike and ax. To the Indians the swivel gun and the air gun were the "big medicine" of the expedition.

York was also of endless interest to the Indians. He entertained them with feats of strength and permitted them to try rubbing off his "black paint." When this pastime became monotonous, he pretended to be ferocious and untamed. Indian women thought that he was a spectacular warrior.

Scannon, Lewis' Newfoundland dog, who weighed 140 pounds, was useful to have along for a trip upriver, for he was a water dog. Still, he must have been weighty baggage for a canoe. On the journey he frequently distinguished

[2] The rifles were half-stock weapons (short) with ribs soldered beneath the barrels, about .52-caliber. The pistols were probably .69-caliber, with walnut stocks, brass mountings, and brass frames, each weighing about three pounds and more than a foot long. The fusils, muskets of a type used by the English, were not very accurate. The blunderbusses were short guns with bell-shaped mouths. The swivel cannon could be turned any direction and was usually loaded with miscellaneous metal pieces. It pivoted on a V bracket which held the barrel. At Fort Mandan such guns were used to defend the stockade. Only one was taken west from Fort Mandan. The air gun was a novelty that Captain Lewis had paid for out of his own pocket. It looked like an ordinary musket. Air was forced into a chamber with bellows, and a large copper ball held back the compressed air until it was released by a trigger. When it was being tested along the Ohio River before the party left St. Louis, it was discharged accidentally and stunned a woman standing forty yards away. Powder for the weapons was packed in lead canisters. There were flints for the rifles, pistols, and fusils.

himself, sometimes for bravery, sometimes for foolishness. He was big enough to kill an antelope swimming in the river and haul it in. Yet when he first met a harmless-looking beaver, he was badly bitten.[3]

On this well-equipped expedition a few items were included that were not ordinarily found on a wilderness journey, among them Cruzatte's violin and the captains' writing desks. The violin survived the journey and made music for dancing around many a campfire. Some of the Indians even said politely that they enjoyed violin music. Clark's desk lasted until September 15, 1805, when one of the pack horses slipped on the perilous Lolo Trail from Montana to Idaho, fell down an embankment, rolled on the desk, and smashed it. That was only one of many accidents. Lewis' desk was cached before the expedition crossed the mountains.

One can imagine that Sacajawea was excited by the trip. She was no longer a prisoner of the Hidatsa tribe that had taken her captive five or six years earlier. Now she was the wife of an interpreter—however few privileges that gave her —and she had a baby. Most important, the expedition was heading toward the land of her birth and her native tribe.

In their entries for the day of departure, April 7, both captains mentioned the Indian girl and her husband. Lewis wrote: "Our party now consists of the following individuals: interpreters George Drewyer and Taussan Charbono; also a black man of the name of York, servant to Captain Clark, and an Indian woman, wife to Charbono, with a young child." Clark, naming the personnel of the party, referred to

[3] On April 26, 1805, Ordway wrote: "Capt Lewises dog Scamon [Scannon] took after [a flock of goats] and caught one in the River."

"Sharbonah and his Indian Squaw to act as interpreter and interpretress for the Snake Indians."

Lewis was optimistic on starting day. He wrote:

Entertaining as I do the most confident hope of succeeding in a voyage which had formed a darling project of mine for the last ten years, I could esteem this moment of departure as among the most happy of my life.

We were about to penetrate a country at least two thousand miles in width on which the foot of civilized man has never trodden.

The Rescue

5

FOR a month the party made fifteen to twenty miles a day. The captains frequently walked on shore, but there were few trees or shrubs for Lewis to examine. The men had some variety in their diet: goose eggs one day, beaver tails and liver another.

Almost immediately Sacajawea proved useful. On April 9 she busied herself in a search for "wild artichokes which the mice collect and deposit in large hordes," as Lewis explained. "This operation she performed by penetrating the earth with a sharp stick about some collection of driftwood. Her labors soon proved successful and she procured a good quantity of these roots."

On April 10, Clark went on foot across a great bend of the Missouri River, taking Charbonneau, Sacajawea, and her baby along. On April 18, Clark walked on shore with Charbonneau, and "the squar followed on with her child." On April 30, Lewis mentioned that Clark spent the greater part of each day walking along the shore accompanied by Charbonneau and Sacajawea. This practice became commonplace.

Having passed the junction of the Yellowstone (near the North Dakota–Montana line) they stopped briefly to celebrate. Each man had one gill of whisky, and all "made merry, fiddled and danced, etc.," Ordway wrote.

May 14 was an exciting day. Both the land and the water parties had hair-raising experiences. The former tried to kill a grizzly bear. Six men, all good hunters, converged on the beast. Four of them fired the first volley, but the bear ran them off a cliff into the river, jumped in after them, and pursued them. When the grizzly was finally killed, eight balls were found to have passed through him.

The water party had enjoyed an easy day. Everything had gone so well that both captains were ashore near the boats when the white pirogue, under full sail, was struck by a sudden squall. Charbonneau was at the helm, although he was, according to Lewis, "the worst steersman of the party" and "perhaps the most timid waterman in the world."

When the wind struck the pirogue, the two captains, looking across three hundred yards of river, saw the craft heel over and then lie agonizingly on her side among the waves. The man handling the brace of the sail clung to it until the wind jerked it out of his hands. The boat was filling as water poured over the gunwale. Charbonneau dropped the tiller and began "crying to his God for mercy" in a scene of wild confusion. Both captains tried to make themselves heard across the water. They fired their rifles, hoping to attract the men's attention. Then Lewis threw down his rifle and shot pouch and was unbuttoning his coat to swim out when he realized that such action would be hopeless.

Cruzatte, in the bow, saved the day by bellowing a threat to shoot Charbonneau if he did not take hold of the rudder and try to right the boat. Cruzatte ordered two of the men to start bailing with kettles. The pirogue did not quite capsize, and the men, hauling in sail, slowly righted her. It was Sacajawea who saved what she could reach of the expedition's valuable supplies. Although burdened with her baby, trying to balance herself in the stern, the Indian girl calmly fished out of the river everything that floated near her. If the pirogue had capsized, the expedition would have been deprived of "nearly everything necessary for our purposes, at a distance of between two and three thousand miles from any place where we could supply the deficiency." Three of the men aboard, including Charbonneau, could not swim.

Lewis, who never became as fond of the Indian girl as Clark did, nevertheless wrote of her glowingly when he related the story of the day in his journal: "The Indian woman, to whom I ascribe equal fortitude and resolution with any person on board at the time of the accident, caught and preserved most of the light articles which were washed overboard."

The pirogue was finally rowed ashore, barely above water, and all the remaining articles were removed from the boat and dried. Apparently the expedition lost chiefly medicines in the accident. Sacajawea probably rescued cases of instruments, compasses, books, clothing—equipment that would float for a time. Many valuable instruments were included in the baggage—spirit levels, a magnet, a quadrant, a sextant, a microscope, a chronometer, a protractor, and platting instruments. There were also valuable books, such as a navigational book, called an ephemeris, giving the daily location of the sun, moon, and planets. Most of the instruments and books were probably packed in waterproof bags and would float briefly. Lewis would have been inconsolable if he had lost his copy of Benjamin Barton's *Elements of Botany*.[1]

Near the junction with the Musselshell River on May 17, three days later, the Corps of Discovery had further excitement. Clark narrowly escaped being bitten by a rattlesnake, and that night their campfire set a large tree ablaze. The trunk burned partly through, and a high wind brought the tree crashing down among the tents. No one was injured.

On May 20, Sacajawea received her first formal recognition: a river was named in her honor. The name, unfortunately, did not endure. As Ordway's journal notes: "With

[1] On one occasion the men upset their lead canisters of powder, but fortunately into shallow water. The canisters were recovered without damage to the contents. Andrew Ellicott, a surveyor, had warned President Jefferson to be sure to have Lewis store the chronometer in a "bladder" when it was not in use, in case a boat overturned.

less gallantry, the present generation call it Crooked Creek."[2]

Although the expedition had not yet encountered any Indians, and were not to see any until they reached the headwaters of the Missouri, there was evidence of Indians here and there—a recently occupied camp, an Indian ball, a moccasin. Sacajawea, who studied the moccasin, said that it did not belong to the Shoshoni.

On the morning of May 29 the party reached the mouth of the Judith River.[3] In the flats around the mouth of the river they found remnants of 126 Indian lodges, but no Indians. Along the bluffs beyond the mouth of the Judith were "buffalo leaps," places where the Indians stampeded buffaloes off the cliffs to their deaths. Lewis wrote that he counted at least one hundred carcasses at the base of the cliffs. The wolves around the carcasses were so tame that Captain Clark was able to kill one with his spontoon.

Next to come in sight along the Missouri were high limestone cliffs that reminded Lewis of "elegant ranges of lofty freestone buildings, having their parapets well stocked with statuary; columns of various sculpture, both grooved and plain."[4]

On June 3 the expedition reached the mouth of a river

[2] This is the first stream that enters the Missouri from the west, above the junction of the Musselshell from the south. Today, because of the widening of the river caused by waters from Fort Peck Dam, it is difficult to determine where the Musselshell entered the big V that the Missouri forms at this point.

[3] Named by Clark for Julia (or Judith) Hancock, of Fincastle, Virginia, whom he later married.

[4] The limestone cliffs decorate the river today just as they did in 1805. The stretch of the Missouri from the Musselshell to Fort Benton is still a primitive region.

flowing from the north. The men stopped there for nine days, while scouting parties went up both branches in an effort to determine which river would lead them to the Rocky Mountains. They named the new-found river the Marias.[5] The Missouri had been uniformly silty, and the Marias looked a good deal like it, but the river coming in from the south (the Missouri, as it proved) ran rapidly and had transparent waters. The captains decided that this branch came from the mountains and was therefore the one to follow. As the expedition left the eroded lands around the Missouri and the outlying rolling prairies, they also left a permanent name for the latter: the Great Plains.

[5] It was Lewis' turn to name a river, and he called it Maria's (the apostrophe has since been dropped). Several other names that Lewis and Clark bestowed on the rivers they discovered were changed by later geographers, for no apparent reason.

Portaging the Falls

6

THE Lewis and Clark Expedition faced a combination of crises after reaching the mouth of the Marias River. From June 3 to July 5 they experienced little but trouble. None of the journals of the expedition, all of which are generally matter-of-fact, really do justice to the men's predicament.

The men reached the Marias nearly exhausted, and exhaustion had spawned illness. They were at a low ebb mentally and physically. Perhaps it was just as well that a rest was taken at the Marias. From the start of the expedition the men had suffered from occasional boils and dysentery. Few days passed with everyone free of illness or injury. Colds, fevers, influenza, abdominal pains, lame backs, nausea, cuts, bruises, and sprains were common. Poor diet and muddy water probably caused some of the sickness. The men were bitten relentlessly by insects. Sometimes the mosquitoes were intolerable, and later gnats, flies, fleas, bugs, and snakes plagued them.

During the long journey to the Pacific Ocean and back, Lewis treated everybody in the party (including himself), for illness or injury, and by the time the return trip started, even Clark had gained a reputation as a doctor. Credit must be given to Captain Lewis for his folk remedies and his bagful of medicines. He hastened the recovery of every sick person on the expedition, despite periodic bleeding of patients and doses of purgatives.

The pause at the Marias was fortuitous for another reason. A mistake in direction at this point might have been fatal to the expedition. Gass, with two others, went up the southern branch, while Pryor, with two men, explored the northern river. For a water expedition the Lewis and Clark troops covered many miles on foot. Sometimes they walked miles away from the river. When Gass and Pryor reported on their exploratory trips, the captains were still uncertain and decided to investigate further. Lewis took a six-man party to explore the Marias, and Clark took five men upriver to the south. Between them they covered one hundred miles, sometimes across the rough country between the two rivers. After the second exploration everybody except the captains themselves thought that the Marias was the main river. Only the two leaders alone were convinced that the south river was the one to follow. As usual, time proved them right.

On June 9 the parties returned to the mouth of the Marias to confer again. It was decided to cache as many supplies as the men could spare,[1] find a hiding place for the red pirogue, and give Captain Lewis and four men time to return from a third exploration of the south branch of the river.

Meanwhile, Sacajawea had fallen ill. Notations in the journals indicate the captains' anxiety about her. They had to take care of her in relays, because first one and then the other captain was away exploring the rivers. On June 11, Lewis, trying to treat the sick girl, also became so unwell that he could not walk. He decided to treat himself, confident of the efficacy of his own concoctions, some of which his mother probably taught him to make.[2] Directing his men to make him a bitter brew of chokecherry twigs, he drank a whole quart of this "strong black decoction" in an hour. The next day he was much improved.

On June 13 Lewis decided to reconnoiter the south branch of the river again. He and four men walked southwest over comparatively level bluffs, overlooking a plain on which many buffaloes were grazing. On the south they saw

[1] A cache was made by digging a bottle-shaped excavation, six or seven feet deep; placing in it the supplies to be recovered later; covering them with turf; and destroying all signs of digging.

[2] Mrs. Lewis was known in Virginia as an "herb doctor."

37

two high buttes. As they continued, they heard a tremendous roar. They realized that they were approaching the Great Falls, which had been described to them by Indians, and that they were indeed on the Missouri River.

Walking another seven miles to the first falls, Lewis wrote, he saw:

Immediately at the cascade, the river is about 300 yards wide. About 90 or 100 yards of this next larboard bluff is a smooth, even sheet of water falling over a precipice of at least 80 feet. The remaining part of about 200 yards on my right forms the grandest sight I ever beheld. The height of the fall is the same as the other, but the irregular and somewhat projecting rocks below receive the water in its passage down, and break it into a perfect white foam which assumes a thousand forms in a moment—sometimes flying up in jets of sparkling foam to the height of 15 to 20 feet; and are scarcely formed before large rolling bodies of the same beaten and foaming water are thrown over and conceal them. In short the rocks seem to be most happily fixed to present a sheet of the whitest beaten froth 200 yards in length and 80 feet perpendicular. The water, after descending, strikes against the butment . . . on which I stand and seems to reverberate; and being met by the more impetuous current, they roll and swell into half-formed billows of great height which rise and again disappear in an instant.

The next day Lewis and his men continued upriver, discovering still more falls. A series of cascades brought the level of the river down about four hundred feet. While separated from his men temporarily, Lewis had one of his many narrow escapes. He encountered a grizzly bear when his gun was unloaded (he had just shot at a buffalo) and was chased into the river. Lewis suddenly turned and faced the bear with his spontoon. The animal wheeled and ran, a typical change of mind peculiar to the grizzly bear.

In the meantime, Clark, who was at the main camp, was trying to cope with Sacajawea's illness and other ailments. On June 12 he wrote: "The interpreter's woman very sick. One man has a felon rising on his hand; the other, with the toothache, has taken cold in the jaw."

The rest of the party was feeling well enough that evening to sing some songs and listen to Cruzatte's violin. But on June 13, Clark noted that Sacajawea was suffering from abdominal pains. Since the weather was turning hot, he laid her in the covered part of the white pirogue, gave her laudanum, and applied bark poultices. Still she grew weaker. When Lewis rejoined the party on June 16, he found the Indian girl extremely ill. He wrote:

About 2 p.m. I reached the camp, found the Indian woman extremely ill, and much reduced by her indisposition. This gave me some concern, as well as for the poor object herself, then with a young child in her arms, as from her condition of her being our only dependence for a friendly negotiation with the Snake Indians [Shoshonis], on whom we depend for horses to assist us in our portage from the Missouri to the Columbia River.

One of the small canoes was left below this rapids in order to pass and repass the river for the purpose of hunting as well as to procure water of the sulphur spring, the virtues of which I now resolved to try on the Indian woman.

... I caused her to drink the mineral altogether.... When I first came down I found that her pulse was scarcely perceptible, very quick; frequently irregular, and attended with strong nervous symptoms; that of the twitching of the fingers and the leaders of the arm; now the pulse has become regular, much fuller, and a gentle perspiration had taken place; the nervous system has also in great measure abated, and she feels herself much freer of pain.

Lewis continued to apply the "cataplasms" (poultices) of bark and laudanum that had previously been used by Captain Clark. "I believe her disorder originated principally from an obstruction of the mensis in consequence of taking could."

Gradually Sacajawea grew better. By June 18 she was sitting up. She soon felt well enough to go out and gather "a considerable quantity of white apples," which she ate, and also a considerable quantity of dried fish. Soon she was sick again, suffering from pain and fever, and Lewis rebuked Charbonneau sharply for letting his wife "indulge herself with food." Yet the next day Sacajawea was better again and celebrated by going fishing. Lewis reported on June 24 that she was fully recovered.

The next crisis was the portage around the series of falls. The men hauled their canoes through water as far upriver as they could go and then set to work to build wagon frames. There was no suitable wood for axles. In fact, they had no material for wheels, and so they cut cross sections of a cottonwood tree, the only one they could find.

The portage of eighteen miles began on June 21, the men pulling their loaded canoes on primitive carts across rough ground carpeted with prickly pear (cactus) that pierced their moccasins and inflamed their feet. Axles cracked; wagon tongues broke. Some of the ground had been crossed and recrossed by thousands of buffaloes, whose rough, scraggy tracks had dried hard as rock.

In the middle of the difficult portage a storm blew up. Captain Clark, Charbonneau, Sacajawea, and her baby were almost swept away by a flood that followed a sudden cloudburst while they were making their way along a creek. Clark exhibited his usual presence of mind, Sacajawea her customary coolness in emergency, and Charbonneau his usual panic. Clark and his small group scrambled for shelter along the riverbank when the heavy rain started. About a fourth of a mile above the falls Clark ordered them under a shelving rock on the upper side of a creek. There was a torrent of rain, and suddenly a wall of water came down the creek.

Clark wrote:

I took my gun and shot pouch in my left hand, and with the right scrambled up the hill pushing the interpreter's wife (who had the child in her arms) before me, the interpreter himself making attempts to pull up his wife by the hand, much scared and nearly without motion. We at length reached the top of the hill safe, where I found my servant in search of us, greatly agitated for our welfare. Before I got out of the bottom of the ravine, which was a flat dry rock when I entered it, the water was up to my waist and wet my watch. I scarcely got out before it raised ten feet deep with a torrent that was terrible to behold, and by the time I reached the top of the hill, at least fifteen feet of water.

The incident was also recorded by Captain Lewis, Gass, and Ordway. Sacajawea lost most of her baby's clothing. Clark lost his compass, and Charbonneau his gun (the compass was later recovered).

The men who had been hauling baggage in the open, hatless and shirtless, were pelted with heavy hailstones. Lewis said some of the stones bounced ten to twelve feet in the air as they landed and that one stone measured seven inches in diameter.

The bruised and battered party finally finished the portage, having spent ten days making eighteen miles, and established camp at White Bear Island. The camp received its name from the "white" (silver-tipped) grizzlies that infested the island and harassed the men in camp.

Now that the two pirogues were cached, Lewis tried to build his famous *Experiment*, the boat whose iron framework they had hauled all the way from the Mississippi River. There was no bark to cover the frame that they assembled and no tar to seal the sewed seams of animal skins that they tried to use instead of bark. The boat began leaking shortly after it was floated, and the project had to be abandoned.

July 4, Independence Day, was celebrated by consuming the last of the supply of whisky, and Cruzatte furnished music on his violin until a heavy shower stopped the concert.

Sacajawea Returns to Home Country

7

WITH the failure of the *Experiment*, Lewis and Clark found it necessary to build two more canoes to supplement the six they already had, all of them hollowed out of cotton-wood logs. After a search through the rather scarce timber they found two cottonwood trees that would serve. They cut them down and built two dugouts, each about three feet wide, one twenty-five and the other thirty-three feet long. Lewis suggested that the men discard some of their souvenirs to avoid overloading the boats. The canoes were ready by July 14. The next day the expedition set out again, going south (upstream) along the eastern edge of the Rockies.

Where were the Indians? Many times they saw "Indian sign," but no Indians. On July 16 some recently occupied willow shelters came into view and, a little farther on, the remains of eighty "leathern lodges."

Despite their preoccupation with Indian sign, the captains did not fail to make notes about the flora and fauna. Lewis wrote in detail about shrubs and berries. To save their parched meal and corn, they subsisted largely on meat and berries.

Some members of the party walked, and some poled and pulled the canoes. Those who were on foot were busy hunting game, but Lewis and Clark alternately looked for Indians. On July 19, Captain Clark passed the site of several Indian camps. Sacajawea, who was walking with Clark, pointed out where the pine trees had been stripped of their bark and explained that the Indians had been hunting for the soft underparts of the wood for food. It was hard walking. Clark reported extracting seventeen cactus needles from his feet that night.

The boats went through the gorge northeast of present-day Helena, Montana, which they named the Gates of the Mountains. On July 20 they emerged into a valley and saw smoke from an Indian camp rising in the distance. The green valley bred hordes of mosquitoes, and they observed that without their "biers" they would have had little sleep.[1]

1 The biers were frameworks for the gauze used to keep off mos-

Sacajawea recognized the countryside on July 22. She said that her tribe made visits to the banks of one of the creeks they were passing to get white earth for paint. The captains named it White Earth Creek. She also told them that the Three Forks of the Missouri were not far away. This news cheered the party.[2]

Captain Clark was still walking energetically, wearing out his companions on the trail. Lewis was helping pole the boats through uncounted islands and around endless bends in the river. He wrote that he had learned "to push a tolerable pole." He wrote of the excessive fatigue of all the party and remarked sadly: "Our trio of pests still invade and obstruct us on all occasions. These are the musquetoes, eye knats and prickley pears, equal to any three curses that ever poor Egypt laiboured under, except the Mahometant yoke."

By July 25, Clark had worn out one companion, Charbonneau, and by the next day Clark was sick himself. But he had finally reached the Three Forks of the Missouri. Several days later the captains decided to name the three rivers after Jefferson and two of the President's cabinet members, Madison and Gallatin.

Clark's ill-health was not improved by having to rescue

quitoes and other insects. They were "like a trunk to get under," Clark wrote. Elliott Coues commented: "Many have thought that Lewis and Clark made too much of these insects, for such brave men as they were. But such critics as these know nothing of mosquitoes." He added that in some areas mosquitoes were so thick they killed horses, cattle, and caribou by clogging the animals' nasal passages.

[2] In January, 1944, C. S. Kingston wrote (in the *Pacific Northwest Quarterly*) that Sacajawea determined the route of the exploring parties on only one occasion (to be discussed later). It should be pointed out, however, that she gave them assurance that they were on the correct route and that she continued to do so on succeeding days.

Charbonneau, who could not swim and was nearly swept away in the current when they waded a stream. By July 27, Clark was so ill that Lewis was administering Dr. Rush's Pills to his friend.[3] In a few days Clark had recovered and was again taking his turn walking on shore or accompanying the canoes.

Lewis wrote: "We begin to feel considerable anxiety with respect to the Snake Indians. If we do not find them or some other nation who have horses, I fear the successful issue of our voyage will be very doubtful."

After investigating the three rivers, a tiresome procedure, the expedition decided that the Jefferson, coming in from the southwest, was the next river to follow. "Our consolation is that this southwest branch can scarcely head with any other river than the Columbia." The captains had a sixth sense when it came to choosing directions, and again they were right, although there were still mountains between them and the Columbia.

The Indian girl reaffirmed that the party had reached Shoshoni ground when she told the captains on July 28 that they were camped on the precise spot where the huts of her people had stood five years before, when the Hidatsas of Knife River first came into sight.

Lewis, with Charbonneau, Sacajawea, and "two invalids," walked along the river and soon found the place where Sacajawea told them the Shoshonis had hidden in the woods when they were attacked. The women and children had fled, leaving Sacajawea and other Indian girls to be captured. She showed them the place where she was over-

[3] Dr. Rush's Pills, like most of the others the captains administered, were a physic.

taken in midriver. Ordway writes: ". . . she was crossing at a shoal place to make hir escape, when caught." Thus the Indian girl who had been taken as a captive all the way to North Dakota had returned with Lewis and Clark to the scenes of her early childhood.

What were her thoughts as she neared the land of her people? "She does not . . . show any distress at these recollections, or any joy at the prospect of being restored to her country," Lewis noted. "For she seems to possess the folly or the philosophy of not suffering her feelings to extend beyond the anxiety of having plenty to eat and a few trinkets to wear." But Sacajawea was more emotional than Lewis suspected, as her reunion with her tribesmen would soon demonstrate.

Where the Jefferson split into three rivers, the captains again had to decide which branch to follow. This time they chose what is now the Beaverhead, the central tributary. On August 8, Sacajawea recognized a high point on the plain on the right, which, she informed the captains, was not far from the summer retreat of her people, on a river flowing west beyond the mountains. She assured them that they would find her people on this river or on the river immediately west of its source, and she also said, correctly, that there were no more falls.

Meeting the Shoshonis

8

THE Lewis and Clark Expedition had been traveling south-ward since leaving the junction with the Marias River in June. It was apparent that they would soon have to turn west. The Missouri had given way to the Jefferson, the Jefferson to the Beaverhead.[1] The information they re-

[1] The ultimate source of the Missouri River is probably upper Red Rock Lake, where Red Rock Creek originates. It flows into the Beaver-

ceived from Sacajawea influenced the decision of the captains to turn toward the mountains on the first tributary of the Beaverhead that looked suitable.

Early in August, Clark was unable to walk very far because of a carbuncle on his ankle. He stayed with the water party while Lewis struck out cross-country with Drewyer (a half-blood French Canadian, who was useful as an interpreter, as well as a hunter), McNeal, and Shields. The Indian girl remained with the canoes.

Lewis was eager to make contact with any Indians he could find. He was reasonably certain that they would be Shoshonis. His hunters had to procure game for food, but their gunshots, Lewis knew, would frighten the Indians. It was necessary to get ahead of the water party, doing as little shooting as possible, so that they could tell the water party where to leave the water and start overland.

The Northern Shoshonis were a tribe of mountain Indians of the Shoshonean linguistic stock. They lived in the mountains because larger enemy tribes overran them whenever they ventured onto the plains. The Shoshonis were not warlike; they had almost no guns. They had fine horses, but even with horses they had difficulty obtaining large game with bows and arrows.[2] The Indians were probably half-

---

head at Dillon, Montana, where the Beaverhead is now considered to terminate.

[2] The Shoshoni horses were probably pintos and Appaloosas. Spanish explorers had brought horses to the southern regions of the United States, and the Indians had traded for them or captured strays. The Shoshonis may have acquired the Appaloosas from their neighbors, the Nez Percés, who were noted for breeding and training them.

A modern-day Indian artist's conception of Sacajawea. The
clothing, decorations, and cradle are close approximations
of Shoshoni dress and ornamentation. The horse's bit is the
leather tie commonly used by Shoshonis and Nez Percés.
Drawing by George Henry, Sioux City, Iowa.

starved, Lewis thought. Why else would they be stripping bark off trees and eating wood fiber?

When he reached the Beaverhead, Captain Lewis, ahead of the water party, decided to turn west on the tributary (later named Horse Prairie Creek) and look for Indian trails. On August 10 he followed the creek for four or five miles toward what is now the Montana–Idaho border and found

a beautiful and extensive plain about 10 miles long and five or six in width. This is surrounded on all sides by higher rolling or waving country, intersected by several little rivulets from the mountains, each bordered by its wide meadows. The whole prospect is bounded by these mountains, which nearly surround it, so as to form a beautiful cover, 16 or 18 miles in diameter.[3]

On the next day, Sunday, August 11, Lewis again set out early with his men to follow Horse Prairie Creek. They headed toward a narrow pass that they saw toward the west, and after walking about five miles, they sighted an Indian on horseback about two miles away. Lewis, studying the horseman through his glass, discerned that he was armed with bow and arrow and was dressed differently from other Indians the explorers had seen. The Indian, he also observed, was riding a good horse.

[3] This area, northwest of present Armstead, Montana, was to be called Shoshoni Cove and was to be an important point on the itinerary of the expedition. It was the camp from which the men searched for and found the Shoshoni Indians and the Continental Divide. Clark would return this way the following year from the Pacific Coast. The junction of Horse Prairie Creek with the Beaverhead was the head of navigation for the party. As soon as Clark's water party reached this junction, the expedition struck out overland.

There followed a dramatic and fruitless confrontation between white man and Shoshoni. As soon as he was near enough, Lewis took out a blanket and spread it out ceremoniously on the ground—a sign of friendship. He moved toward the Indian, waving a looking glass, beads, and other trinkets. Then he shouted "Ta-ba-bone," an Indian word which meant "white man" but probably did not have an equivalent in Shoshoni. Drewyer and Shields unfortunately kept moving around to each side of the Indian. Lewis' signals to them to stop went unheeded. The Indian reined in and watched all three uncertainly. Then he suddenly wheeled his horse, leaped a creek, and disappeared in the willows.

The men were gloomy that night. They set out the next day, following what appeared to be an Indian trail. Horse Prairie Creek divided, and they followed Trail Creek. They found signs indicating that the Indians had been digging up roots, and they continued on, tramped across high ground, and descended the other side. They had just surmounted the Continental Divide at Lemhi Pass. The ridge they crossed is now the boundary line between Montana and Idaho.

Lewis reports what he saw:

. . . I discovered immense ranges of high mountains still to the west of us, with their tops partially covered with snow. I now descended the mountain about three quarters of a mile, which I found much steeper than the opposite side, to a handsome bold running creek of cold, clear water. Here I first tasted the water of the great Columbia River.[4]

[4] It is now called the Lemhi River, a tributary of the Salmon and the Salmon of the Snake, before the Snake enters the Columbia. Lewis

Having killed nothing that day, the men ate a little of their remaining provisions (pork, flour, and parched meal) and found some currants. Early on the morning of August 13 they resumed their march along the Indian trail, found another creek, a tributary of the Lemhi River, proceeded along a rolling plain, and saw at a distance two Indian women, a man, and a few dogs. All were wary, disappearing before Lewis could reach them.

The dusty path led them unexpectedly upon two women and a little girl. The younger woman fled. The old woman and the little girl, perhaps feeling that they could not escape, sat quietly with bowed heads, expecting death. Captain Lewis spoke to them gently, producing presents, and asked the woman to call back the young woman. She did so, and Lewis distributed more presents and painted their cheeks with vermilion, to the Shoshonis emblematic of peace.

The women led Lewis and his men toward their camp, and soon about sixty warriors rode up to them. The chief spoke to the women, who told them that the white men were friends, and soon Captain Lewis was being enthusiastically embraced, cheek to cheek, as the Indians called out "Ah-hi-e! Ah-hi-e!" an exclamation of friendship. Lewis remarks, "We were all caressed and besmeared with their grease paint until I was heartily tired of the national hug."

There followed a pipe-smoking ceremony and distribution of a few gifts. Then everyone went to the Indian camp,

had crossed Lemhi Pass, and he and his men would camp on the western slope. The Lemhi River was so named in 1855, when Mormons established a settlement there (abandoned in 1858). The Mormon colony did not cross Lemhi Pass. They reached the area by way of Ogden, Utah, and Idaho Falls.

about four miles away, for more ceremonies. Drewyer, using sign language, served as interpreter during the conference that followed. Asked about the course of the Lemhi River, the Indians told Lewis that neither it nor the river into which it flowed was navigable. If this was true, Lewis realized, the party must obtain horses.

While these events were taking place, Captain Clark's party was toiling up the Beaverhead. The river was so crooked and full of shoals that progress was painfully slow. Lewis had to think of some way to convince the Indians that the men coming upriver were friendly, that they had a Shoshoni Indian girl with them, and that their hunters would kill some much-needed game. Both the Indians and Lewis' men were very hungry. The Shoshonis were valiantly trying to procure meat with their bows and arrows, and it was obvious to Captain Lewis that before he could discuss the purchase of horses he must produce something to eat. He sent out Drewyer and Shields on two borrowed horses, but to Lewis' embarrassment they returned with no game. The next day Lewis divided his few remaining provisions among some of the Indian chiefs.

Cameahwait, the head chief of the Shoshonis, was friendly to the white men. A few of the lesser chiefs and a good many warriors, however, were suspicious of the explorers and their story of a party coming up the Beaverhead. Were the white men in league with their Indian enemies? Lewis finally persuaded some of the warriors to accompany him back to the river fork, where he hoped Clark's party was waiting.

Drewyer and Shields went hunting again, this time with suspicious Indians trailing them. There was a stroke of luck:

Drewyer killed a deer. An Indian came galloping back happily to tell the others. Lewis, who could not see what the excitement was about, was carrying a young Indian behind him on his horse. The Indian boy, who wanted something to eat, lashed the animal at every jump for a whole mile before the captain could discover where everyone was hurrying.

The meat-starved Indians had a bloody feast at the spot where the deer was killed—devouring the meat and entrails raw. When two more deer were killed, Lewis' problems were partly solved.

The river party had not yet arrived at the fork, however. The men with Clark had found the river ever shallower and swifter. Ordway complained: "The water is very cold. We have to waid in it, which makes our feet and legs ake with cold. We expect it is made of springs."

On August 15 Clark's party passed two tall rock pillars, which they named Rattlesnake Clifts because they were crawling with snakes. Both Clark and Sacajawea narrowly escaped being bitten.

In the valley beyond, Sacajawea picked some serviceberries. Clark saw that they were approaching a fork in the river. He, Charbonneau, and the Indian girl walked through high, dew-covered grass, Clark behind because he was still lame. Suddenly he saw Sacajawea jump up and down, dancing, sucking her fingers, and pointing to Indians riding toward her.

"This is my tribe!" she was saying in sign language, as she danced ecstatically. Sacajawea had returned to her people.

Clark describes the reunion of the Indian girl with her people:

... I saw at a distance several Indians on horseback coming towards me. The interpreter and the squaw who were before me at some distance danced for the joyful sight, and she made signs to me that they were her nation. As I approached nearer them, I discovered one of Captain Lewis's party with them dressed in their dress. They met me with great signs of joy.

This meeting took place near present-day Armstead, Montana. In the Biddle edition of the journals appears a description of the conference which followed:

While Sacajawea was renewing among the women the friendships of former days, Captain Clark went on, and was received by Captain Lewis and the chief, who, after the first embraces and salutations were over, conducted him to a sort of circular tent or shade of willows. Here he was seated on a white robe, and the chief immediately tied in his hair six small shells resembling pearls, an ornament highly valued by these people, who procured them in the course of trade from the sea-coast. The moccasins of the whole party were then taken off, and after much ceremony, the smoking began. After this the conference was to be opened. ... Sacajawea was sent for. She came into the tent, sat down, and was beginning to interpret, when, in the person of Cameahwait, she recognized her brother. She instantly jumped up, and ran and embraced him, throwing over him her blanket, and weeping profusely. The chief himself was moved, though not in the same degree. After some conversation between them she resumed her seat and attempted to interpret for us; but her new situation overpowered her, and she was frequently interrupted by her tears.

After the council was finished the unfortunate woman

learned that all her family were dead except two brothers, one of whom was absent, and a son by her eldest sister, a small boy, who was immediately adopted by her.

After the canoes arrived, chiefs, warriors, and members of the expedition met again for the customary smoking ceremony, where the captains spoke at some length, asking for horses to transport their equipment across the mountains, as well as for a guide. More presents were distributed—Jefferson medals, shirts, tobacco, and small articles. The air gun was shot off. Everything surprised the Indians—the appearance of the men, their arms, their clothing, the canoes, Clark's Negro servant, even the intelligence of Scannon, the dog. The hunters brought in four more deer and antelope.

On Sunday, August 18, the party traded for a few horses, and Clark set out to discover whether the Lemhi River was indeed unnavigable, as the Indians had said. Gass wrote in his diary:

A fine morning. We bought three horses of the Indians. Captain Clark and 11 more, with our interpreter and his wife and all the Indians, set out at 11 o'clock to go over to the Columbia [Lemhi]. The Indians went for horses to carry our baggage, and we to search for timber to make canoes for descending the Columbia.

On the same day Lewis wrote (poignantly, in retrospect, in view of his death at thirty-five in 1809):

This day I completed my thirty-first year, and conceived that I had in all human probability now existed about half the period which I am to remain on this sublunary world. I reflected that I had as yet done but little . . . to further the happiness of the human race. . . . I viewed with regret the many hours I have spent in indolence . . . but since they are past and cannot be recalled, I dash from me the gloomy thought and resolve in the future to redouble my exertions . . . or, in the future to live for mankind, as I have heretofore lived for myself.

Across the Divide to the Columbia

9

SACAJAWEA was elated by the reunion with her tribe. She had found a brother, Cameahwait, and her sister's son. She had been reunited with the girlhood companion who had been captured with her by the Hidatsas. (Unlike Sacajawea, this girl had escaped and made her way back to her tribe.)[1]

[1] During the stay with the Shoshonis, Sacajawea also encountered a

Yet despite her joy at being reunited with her people, it is apparent that Sacajawea's loyalties had been committed to the white men. Although she doubtless could have stayed with the Shoshonis, she chose to remain with Charbonneau and the expedition. She would go on to the Pacific with them.

It was decided that Clark would explore the Lemhi River to determine whether it was navigable. Before he left, he took Sacajawea and Charbonneau to the main Shoshoni camp to help hasten the collecting of horses.[2] Clark and eleven of the men were to build canoes, if the condition of the river and the supply of trees made it practicable. The captains suspected, however, that a portage of the Rocky Mountains would be necessary. They bartered for three horses before Clark's reconnaissance party set out.

Chief Cameahwait drew diagrams of the rivers for Clark. Although his information was vague and communication difficult, he indicated that the Lemhi River flowed into the Salmon, the Salmon into the Snake, the Snake into the Columbia, and the Columbia into the Pacific.

-----

warrior who declared that in early childhood she had been promised to him as a wife. But upon learning that she was married to Charbonneau and had a son by him, the Indian renounced his claim to her.

[2] By her presence Sacajawea undoubtedly helped the expedition secure horses from her people, just as she undoubtedly helped maintain cordial relations between the captains and the chiefs. The Shoshonis had about seven hundred horses at this time, but the bartering situation was precarious because the items the Shoshonis wanted most —trade goods, guns, and ammunition—the men of the Lewis and Clark party did not have. They could only make small gifts, give speeches, and promise future trade between white men and the Shoshonis.

From August 19 to 26, Clark and his men investigated the Lemhi and Salmon rivers, finding them just as forbidding as the Indians had described them. The circle trip along the Lemhi and Salmon and back amounted to about seventy miles of rugged country. By August 24, Clark had decided that they should not try to take a water route.[3] The situation was serious, because fall was approaching and there was little game. The men would have to start soon.

By now the members of the expedition were used to hardships, as their journals frequently pointed out. But they were not used to going without food for days at a time or subsisting on only a few berries or roots or small fish, their present diet. The Shoshonis were on a meager diet too. Cameahwait pronounced a piece of dried squash which the expedition had brought from Mandan country, the best food he had ever tasted—except for sugar, a small lump of which Sacajawea had saved and given to him.

While Clark was on his reconnaissance, Lewis was trying to barter for horses with Indians who were more interested in hunting. Three deer, brought in on August 25 by his men, alleviated the food shortage temporarily, but on the same day Lewis had a bad scare. Sacajawea had told Charbonneau that all the Shoshoni hunters were leaving for buffalo country the next day. With his usual dull-wittedness, Charbonneau failed to relay this information to Lewis until that afternoon.

Lewis could foresee the results of such a caprice: he and his men would be left stranded in the mountains. He called together the three main chiefs and asked them whether they

[3] In 1893, Coues wrote: "Perhaps Captain Clark's good judgment in abandoning any route by way of the Salmon River saved the expedition."

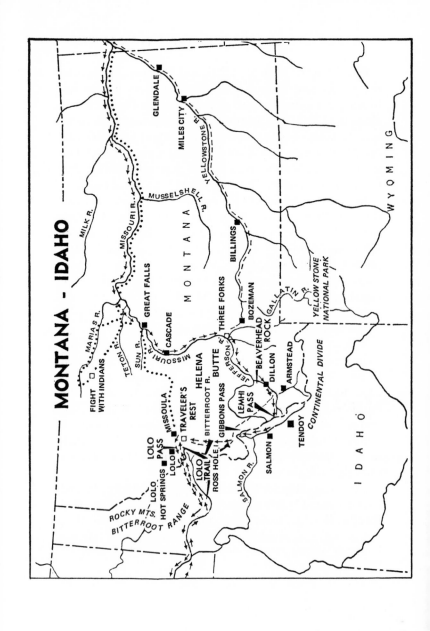

MONTANA - IDAHO

MONTANA—IDAHO

On the westward trip the Lewis and Clark Expedition followed the Missouri River to Three Forks and then followed the river they named the Jefferson, (the most westerly branch of the three forks. They continued up the Beaverhead (the higher part of the Jefferson), branched off westward at Horse Prairie Creek, crossed Lemhi Pass, and entered the present state of Idaho. They crossed a mountain pass back into Montana, following the Lemhi River and the Bitterroot to what is now Missoula, Montana, where they turned west through Lolo Pass, followed the high "buffalo trail" of the Nez Percés, recrossed the Bitterroots again, came down into a broad, flat prairie, and again began traveling by water at the forks of the Clearwater near Lewiston, Idaho.

On their return trip they divided near Missoula, Lewis and his men going northeast to Great Falls, thence on an exploratory tour of the Marias River, turning back to the junction of the Marias with the Missouri after a skirmish with Blackfoot Indians. Clark and his men went southward in Montana, through Gibbon's Pass, back to the Beaverhead, crosscountry eastward at Three Forks to the Yellowstone, and down that river to its junction with the Missouri.

were men of their word. He reminded them of their promise to help his party cross the mountains. Cameahwait finally admitted that he was wrong, excusing himself by saying that his people were hungry. Lewis must have breathed a sigh of relief when on the next day, August 26, Cameahwait promised him at least twenty more horses.

"I directed the fiddle to be played," Lewis wrote, "and the party danced very merrily, much to the amusement and gratification of the natives, though I must confess that the state of my own mind at this moment did not well accord with the prevailing mirth."

By August 29, Lewis and Clark had bargained for twenty-nine horses, none in especially good flesh. The party then set out, accompanied by an old Indian guide, Toby, his four sons, and another Indian who went along out of curiosity. They started north along the Lemhi River. By September 2 all the Indians but their guide and one of his sons had left them. Progress had become extremely difficult. The horses, carrying baggage, frequently slipped and fell down the rocky slopes. One was crippled, two worn out. It was not an auspicious start.[4]

Bad weather was expected momentarily and it was no surprise when, on September 3, snow began to fall. Soon the surrounding mountaintops were white. The men shivered in the cold. They had broken their last thermometer and could not take temperature readings. About two inches of snow fell. Then it rained, and the rain turned to sleet.

[4] The party was now in the vicinity of present-day Gibbonsville, Idaho, a small town in the tip of the eastern bulge of lower Idaho. They were barely west of the Continental Divide, approaching Lost Trail Pass.

"We crossed a high mountain!" the journals exclaim on September 4, reporting the second crossing of the Bitterroot Range, a chain of mountains four hundred miles long. The men had crossed from Idaho back into Montana, traveling north.

In Ross's Hole, a wide valley, they encountered a large camp of Flathead Indians. Lewis and Clark called them Ootlashoots. They looked much like the Shoshonis and dressed a good deal like them, but their language puzzled the white men, who described it as like the "clucking of the fowl" or the "noise of a parrot." The Flatheads were friendly, shared berries and roots, and sold the expedition eleven more horses.

By the evening of September 7 the Corps of Discovery had progressed northward along the Bitterroot River to a point near present Grantsdale, Montana. They noted many creeks coming into the river, but not until September 9, when they reached a large creek joining the Bitterroot River on the west side, did their Indian guide notify them that the time had come to turn west. The explorers described the stream that they would follow as a "fine bold creek of clear water, about 20 yards wide, which we call Traveler's Rest creek." There they stayed two days, hunting and repairing clothing. From this point (Lolo) they would turn toward the Pacific Ocean over what came to be known as the Lolo Trail.

The men started up Traveler's Rest Creek on September 11. The valley grew narrower. Next day they made a difficult short cut across steep, stony hills to avoid the bends of the stream, and on Friday, September 13, they found some hot springs.[5] On that day the party had its share of bad luck: Lewis lost his horse, and Toby, the guide, mistakenly took them three miles out of the way on "an exceedingly bad route" before he found the right trail again. On that day they crossed the main divide of the Bitterroot Mountains and passed over from Montana again into what is now Idaho. It was their third crossing of the range. The expedition's drooping spirits were buoyed by the end of the day by the deer and several grouse that their hunters killed.

The main journals of the party are worded so tersely that it is difficult to imagine the agonizingly slow and painful progress across the mountains. Only occasionally do comments by some of the diarists reveal their sufferings. Gass described the terrain as a "horrible mountain desert." Ordway complained: "We eat our verry last morcil of our provisions except a little portable soup."[6] Later he entered: "We killed a wolf and eat it."

On Sunday, September 15, several of the packhorses lost their footing on the treacherous trail. One horse, carrying Clark's desk, rolled on top of it and smashed it. Despite these crises the headwaters of the Kooskooskie (Clearwater) River were reached that day.

Journal entries such as the following give a bleak picture of the next few days:

It began to snow and continued all day. . . . We were obliged to kill a second colt for our supper. . . . Our guns are scarcely of any service, for there is no living creature in these mountains except a few small pheasants [grouse], a small species

[5] Lolo Hot Springs.
[6] A dehydrated mixture which nobody liked and which was eaten only as a last resort.

of gray squirrel and a blue bird . . . about the size of a turtle dove or jay. . . . One of our horses slipped and rolled over with his load down the hillside. . . . The men are growing weak and losing their flesh very fast.

Clark, with an advance hunting party, named one stream Hungry Creek because there they had nothing to eat.

Such conditions prevailed until September 20. Clark's party, and later the other explorers, descended with relief out of the ridges and reached Weippe Prairie, the favorite camas-root grounds of the Indians of the region. The plains were dotted with lodges of the Nez Percés.[7]

These Indians seemed well disposed, and on September 21, Captain Lewis made the acquaintance of Chief Twisted Hair. The chief gave Lewis the impression of being "cheerful and sincere."[8] The captains held a conference two days later and passed out more gifts and Jefferson medals. Great crowds of Indians gathered around.

There was more food in the region—camas roots, berries, and dried fish. On his map of 1814, Clark labeled this low

[7] Nez Percé is French for "pierced nose." Fur traders observed some members of the tribe wearing shells in their noses. The route the party had taken was known as the "upper Nez Percé buffalo trail," along the ridges of the mountains. Today a modern highway follows the route, but at a lower altitude. Since the days of Lewis and Clark the high ridges have been traversed by men with pack horses— all of whom have found the passage difficult. In recent years snowmobiles have tried the trail. The drivers are faced with the same problem that challenged Lewis and Clark—staying on the ridges.

[8] Apparently the captains thought that the Nez Percés were friendly from the start, but Indian tradition describes the tribe as suspicious of white men. These Indians apparently thought seriously of waylaying and killing the white men as they straggled through the mountains, but were dissuaded by an aged Indian woman, Stray Away, who had once been befriended by a white trader.

69

country Quamash (Camas) Flats. The change from a meat diet, together with the temptation to eat too much, made most of the explorers sick.[9] In an effort to restore some meat to their diet, the whites bought dogs from the Indians.[10]

A spell of hot weather followed the cold. It was not until October 3 that the men had sufficiently recovered from the trip to go to work. Cool winds on that day and the next helped. Captain Lewis, who had also been ill, could walk around a little by then.

The hunters tried to find game to shoot, and others of the party who felt well enough worked on canoes. They conserved their energy by burning out the tree trunks, Indian style. This spot was called Canoe Camp, at the forks of the "upper" and "lower" Clearwater River (about five miles west of present-day Orofino, Idaho), a stream that probably carried much more water in those days than it does now.

On October 6 the men of the expedition hid their saddles, along with some powder and bullets, branded their horses with an iron stirrup, and arranged for the Nez Percés to keep the animals until their return. The next day one small canoe and four large ones were loaded, and water travel once more was resumed. Old Toby, the Indian guide, had no fondness for this form of travel. He left, without collecting his pay.

On the night of October 9, as the explorers camped near

[9] Camas roots, eaten without other food, were both an emetic and a purgative to anyone whose stomach was not accustomed to them.

[10] Neither the Shoshonis nor the Nez Percés, although they sold dogs to the members of the expedition, cared about eating dog meat. Tradition says that Sacajawea was never hungry enough to partake of it.

the junction of the Clearwater and Snake rivers, the Indians gave them a final, noisy going-away party.[11]

[11] The white men, as usual, danced for the Indians, whose descendants could still describe the scene in the 1930's. Potts, whose monosyllabic name was easy for the Indians to remember, was apparently a star performer: "He boss other mans how to do funny dance and sing songs, all laugh" (apparently Potts called the figures for a square dance). "Negro York he do lots dance with feet and looks funny." John Bakeless, *Lewis and Clark: Partners in Discovery,* 268.

Past the Cascades of the Columbia

10

IT was to be expected that the voyage, downstream from now on, would be easy, without need for poles, towlines, or portages. That was the optimistic hope the members of the expedition held when they set off down the Clearwater River. There were some surprises in store for them.

At first the canoes floated down the river serenely, but soon they came to rapids. One of the canoes hung itself on a rock, and the men spent an hour disengaging it. That was just the beginning. The next day they passed the junction of the Clearwater and the Snake and encountered still more rapids.

Down the Snake and the Columbia the story was the same. Mileage was sure to be good each day, provided the canoes could survive the endless series of rapids. Many of the Indians the explorers met along the way were friendly, but some were terrified by the appearance of the strangers. When the Indians were frightened, they usually hid, but were soon reassured by seeing Sacajawea with her baby.

Along this river the staple of Indian diet was salmon, and along the banks the men saw groups of Indians drying fish. There were a few Indians on horseback and many in canoes. The latter obviously knew how to negotiate the rapids.

On October 14 three of the explorers' canoes hit rocks in the river. Cargoes spilled into the water, and one crew was forced to perch on a rock until rescued. Bedding and tomahawks were lost. Canisters of powder were dredged up from the riverbed. To dry out their baggage, the men had to break one of their rules—not to touch Indian property— "borrowing" a little split wood from an Indian cache to build a fire.

Three days later they reached the confluence of the Snake and the Columbia. They judged the Columbia to be 960 yards wide at that point, soon widening to a distance of one to three miles. There they found a tribe of Indians they called the Sokulks, who, along with most of the other tribes living along the river, fished in the glare of the sun and gazed constantly on snow in winter and consequently had chronically inflamed eyes. Those who subsisted chiefly on fish also had bad teeth, Lewis noted.

On October 19 the party met Chief Yellepit. He was perhaps a chief of the Cayuse Indians; the explorers referred to him as "the head of a band on the river below." He was a particularly intelligent and respected chief, "35 years of age, with a bold and dignified countenance." They would see him again the following spring.

On the same day they navigated Umatilla Rapids and saw Mount Adams and Mount Hood in the distance. Also on the same day Captain Clark unintentionally frightened a group of Indians. While rowing over to some houses along the shore, he shot a duck and a white crane, both of which fell into the water near the houses. It took him some time to convince the thirty-two terrified men, women, and children of the village that a man with so much magic at his command was friendly, especially when he took out his "burning glass" and, without thinking, lit his pipe. In the end presents pacified the Indians.

The next day, more rapids. They became an almost daily menace. On October 21, J. Collins presented the party with some acceptable beer that he had brewed from a bread made from roots. The explorers reached Celilo Falls on October 22 and portaged twelve hundred yards, descending more than thirty feet in two days, dropping their boats with elk-skin ropes over large rocks. At the upper end of the portage were new enemies—fleas. Waste left behind by Indians who had camped there had nourished a multitude of insects, which, the journals noted, "were so pleased to exchange the straw and fish skins . . . for some better residence, that we were soon covered with them."

On October 24 the party escaped destruction while bringing canoes and baggage successfully through six miles of rapids and whirlpools (the Short Narrows, forty-five yards wide), to the astonishment of the Indians below. The Indians there (Echeloots, or Wishrams) had the largest supply of dried salmon Lewis and Clark had yet seen, over ten thousand pounds. Most of the river Indians did not want to barter fish that they needed, and the explorers were not especially fond of fish anyway. They preferred to subsist on whatever they could shoot or on dogs they could buy. The Indians were willing to exchange dogs for such small articles as bells, thimbles, brass wire, and beads. They also prized fishhooks and needles.

On the next day the expedition encountered the Long Narrows. There the three-mile-long river channel, worn through hard, rough, black rock, was only fifty to one hundred yards wide. "The water swells and boils in a tremendous manner," it was noted. A canoe was damaged running this narrows. The men portaged most of their valuable stores and at last emerged into a fairly quiet basin. The campsite that night was a high point of rocks, which they named Fort Rock Camp (for the flat rocks forming the bed of the river, now called (The Dalles). It appeared that hunting, and consequently diet, might improve. Moreover, the men saw a deer, a goose, a beaver, and a sea otter—clearly the coast was near.

At this point along the Columbia were several Indian tribes, most of them friendly and helpful.[1] The Indians

[1] One of the men shot a goose that fell into the river. An Indian plunged into the channel, swam close to the rocks, where he could have been dashed to pieces, seized the goose, and swam to shore "with

knew a few English words and had learned to ask high prices for the few items they were willing to sell. Obviously they had had contact with men from trading ships.

Alternately quiet and noisy water appeared in the river as the expedition proceeded down the Columbia. At the "Great Shoot," the Cascades of the Columbia, it was wisely decided to portage, since the river was confined for a quarter of a mile within 150 yards and then dropped steeply over rocks in a 20-foot fall.[2] A mile and a half further on, the river was again confined within a narrow channel between large rocks. Unloaded canoes were sent down the second series of cascades on November 2, and a note was later made that this was the "last of all the descents of the Columbia." Camp was made twenty-nine miles farther down, on the Oregon side, at the edge of the Willamette Valley.

A little farther upriver on the Washington shore a perpendicular rock about eight hundred feet high created much interest. It was named Beacon Rock.[3] The explorers' first Oregon camp was somewhat more than halfway from the Cascades to the present city of Portland.

great composure." The men willingly gave the Indian the bird. He plucked about half the feathers and then, without opening the goose, ran a stick through it and carried it off to be roasted.

[2] The Cascades were the first series of rapids on the Columbia to be dammed and to furnish hydroelectric power. Other large dams on the river below the Snake are John Day, Bonneville, and McNary.

[3] Beacon Rock is perhaps the best-known landmark on the Columbia, standing at the head of tidewater and visible for some twenty miles below. Clark at first spelled it Beaten Rock.

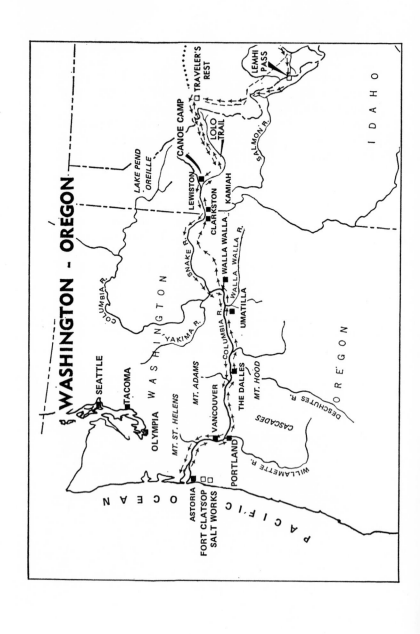

WASHINGTON—OREGON

Except for a few variations, the Lewis and Clark party followed the same route westward to the Pacific Coast and then back through Washington, after spending the winter at Fort Clatsop on the Oregon coast. From the forks of the Clearwater in Idaho to the Pacific Ocean near Astoria, they took the water route—the Clearwater, Snake, and Columbia rivers.

The Canoe Camp was at the forks of the Clearwater. There the men made dugout canoes after portaging the mountains on horseback and by foot. Beside the old trail near Canoe Camp stumps of trees from which the canoes were made were still being pointed out as late as 1900.

Camping on the Columbia

11

FROM this point on, the explorers would camp at relatively close distances along the upward bend of the Columbia, until they finally decided on November 24 to try the south side for a permanent winter camp. There was little promise of finding trading ships near the mouth of the Columbia.

They camped on the Oregon side on November 3, discovering that new obstacles and hardships awaited them.

The fog was so thick that they could not make out anything at a distance of fifty steps. They tried to wade across the mouth of the Sandy River, which joined the Columbia, only to discover that its bars were quicksand. They hastily returned to their canoes.

Nearly every day Indians came into camp to trade and observe the whites at work. One group brought with them a female prisoner who was supposedly Shoshoni. Sacajawea was introduced to her, but the two women could not understand each other. The prisoner had probably been taken captive by the Shoshonis from some other tribe.

Captain Lewis thought that some of the Indians' mode of dress, especially that of the women, was so unusual that he described it in detail:

The women are clad in a peculiar manner, the robe not reaching lower than the hip, and the body being covered in cold weather by a sort of corset of fur, curiously plaited and reaching from the arms to the hip; added to this is a sort of petticoat, or rather tissue of white cedar bark, bruised or broken into small strands, and woven into a girdle. . . . Being tied around the middle, these strands hang down as low as the knee in front, and to the mid-leg behind; they are of sufficient thickness to answer the purpose of concealment whilst the female is in an erect position, but in any other attitude form but a very ineffectual defense.

One day an Indian wearing a sailor's jacket offered to pilot them down the channel. Now the distant roar of breakers could be heard, and on November 7, after the fog cleared, they were charmed by the "mountainous high country" along the right bank. By nightfall it was raining again. Their camp that night was opposite a high rock in the water (Pillar Rock). High mountains could be seen in the southwest.

On November 8 the ocean was sighted. "Great joy in camp," wrote the usually unemotional Clark. "We are in view of the Ocian, this great Pacific Octian which we have been so long anxious to see, and the roreing or noise made by the waves brakeing on the rockey shores (as I suppose) may be heard disti[n]ctly." The estimated distance the explorers had traveled from St. Louis to the ocean was 4,100 miles.

Throughout the rest of the month the explorers moved uncertainly along the northern shore of the Columbia, trying to find a suitable site for a winter camp. It is natural to think of the Columbia as a wide, placid stream whose mouth could be explored at will under pleasant conditions. But at that time of year the river was whipped into high waves by the winds. Fogs shrouded the water, and debris was driven against the northern shoreline, where precipitous banks alternated with spits, points, and what Clark picturesquely called "nitches." Rain fell almost constantly. Few campsites were safe. The expanding mouth of the river varied from five to ten miles in width, depending upon what could actually be called the mouth.[1]

Conditions were wretched all through the month of November. The salty river water was almost undrinkable.

[1] Because the vast mouth of the Columbia is shrouded much of the time in fog, its discovery by Pacific mariners was delayed for some years—they sailed right by it. In 1791, Robert Gray, a Yankee shipmaster, found a bay into which an unknown river was discharging a current so strong that he could not ascend it. Again in 1792 he found the mouth and named it the Columbia after his ship. He also gave the name Cape Hancock to what is now Cape Disappointment.

The hills bordering the river were so steep that there was no storage place for the men's baggage at night. If the dugouts were left in the water, the waves dashed them against the shore and threatened to break them up. High tides washed in immense floating trees. Firewood was almost impossible to find. The men's clothes, tents, and baggage rotted in the rain.

More out of curiosity than a desire to help, small groups of Indians continued to visit the expedition from time to time by canoe. The Indians had lighter, more maneuverable canoes than those of the white party. "Those Indians are the best canoe navigators I ever saw," commented Clark.

Young females, blatantly offering to sell themselves to the men of the expedition, became a nuisance. The captains would have liked to obtain Indian goods, especially foods, but the natives wanted exorbitant prices. Usually they demanded blue, or "chief," beads, which all the coast Indians coveted, but unfortunately the expedition had exhausted its supply of blue beads. One visiting Indian had a gorgeous sea-otter robe that the captains were determined to secure. Sacajawea gave up her belt of blue beads so that a trade could be made for the robe. In compensation she was given a coat of blue cloth.

The captains finally reached the conclusion that the northern banks of the river were too unfriendly for occupation and that winter camp should be pitched somewhere else, perhaps on the south side. On November 26 they made a crossing, retreating fifteen miles upstream before finding a suitable place to paddle to the southern shore.

The decision to cross the Columbia had been duly voted upon by the whole party, including York and Sacajawea.

The Indian girl said that she favored going where there were "plenty of potatoes"—by which she meant wapatoo, an edible root.

Though the rain was heavy on the south side of the river, game was more plentiful there. Lewis, with three men, went on a three-day reconnaissance and found the elk abundant. Sacajawea showed the men what could be done with an elk after the meat had disappeared. She "broke two shank bones of the elk after the marrow was taken out; boiled them and extracted a pint of grease or tallow from them."

According to Gass, at length Lewis found a place for winter camp "about 15 miles from this camp, up a small river which puts into a large bay." The bay was named Meriwether's Bay, and to reach it the expedition rounded Smith's Point, on which Astoria was later founded. Living in this vicinity were various families from a group of Clatsop Indians. They were much neater in their persons and eating habits than most of the Indians the explorers had seen. Lewis and Clark got on well with them, and here they decided to build winter quarters—a fortification that they would call Fort Clatsop. The party moved to the new site on December 7.[2]

The men built eight cabins on high ground, avoiding the low areas, which were swampy. The cabins, each sixteen by thirty feet, were surrounded by a stockade. In one of the cabins was a tree stump so large that it could not be re-

[2] Before they moved, Clark autographed a pine tree with his famous legend: "William Clark December 3rd 1805. By land from the U. States in 1804 and 1805" (the United States was then considered to end at the Mississippi River). The party was outside the Louisiana Purchase from the time they left Montana.

moved. The men built around it, and Clark used it as a writing desk and drafting table.

The fort was nearly completed by Christmas. The men held a party and exchanged presents. Clark happily noted in his journal that he received fleece hosiery, shirt, drawers, and socks from Captain Lewis; a pair of "mockersons" from Whitehouse, and "two dozen white weazil tails" from Sacajawea. The Christmas feast consisted of little but "pore elk," however. Meanwhile, the fleas were still active, and the rain continued to fall.

By January 1 the winter quarters were finished—as snug as could be hoped for in that far outpost. The members of the expedition settled down to spend what was to be a winter of dampness, beautiful scenery, and skimpy diet. It was for the most part a monotonous winter. The men spent their time repairing gear, collecting salt, and striking up acquaintances with the Clatsop Indians and their likable chief, Yanakasac Coboway, whose name the captains rendered as Comowool. The fort was operated in military style, with sentries always on duty.

Winter at Fort Clatsop

12

"O! how disagreeable is our Situation dureing this dreadful weather," Clark complained.

The winter at Fort Clatsop was not severe, only miserable. At the first of the new year, 1806, a goodly number of the men were sick. Even York was ill with a cold from the strain of "carrying meat from the woods and lifting the heavy logs."

FORT CLATSOP

Southwest of Astoria, Oregon, where Lewis and Clark wintered in 1805–1806

Still, there were diversions. With ocean water available, a group of the men established an evaporation plant on a fine beach just north of present-day Tillamook Head. They boiled water in kettles, scraping salt from them and storing twenty gallons in iron-bound kegs.[1] "I care little wheather I have any with my meat or not," Clark observed, but most of the men found the salt a great treat.

One day the Indians who came to observe the salt workers reported that a large whale had been cast upon the shore of the ocean. Sacajawea, in one of her few recorded complaints, said that she had traveled a long way to see the

[1] A pile of rocks near the site, not far from Seaside, Oregon, is one of the few remaining physical signs of the expedition.

great waters and, now that a monstrous fish was also to be seen, she thought it "very hard" that she could not be permitted to see it, and the ocean too.

Sacajawea's complaint fell on sympathetic ears, and Clark took her, Charbonneau, and a group of men in two canoes to find the whale and, if possible, obtain some blubber. The explorers descended Tillamook Head, crossing an eighty-yard-wide stream, which they named Ecola, or Whale Creek. Tillamook Head and nearby Cannon Beach were the southernmost coastal points the expedition reached. By the time the men found the whale, all that remained of the monster was a skeleton, Clark ruefully noted. The Indians had almost stripped the bones. Clark and his party procured about three hundred pounds of blubber from the Indians, which they had to haul thirty-five miles back to Fort Clatsop. One member of the group, McNeal, nearly came to grief on the return trip as he was passing through an Indian village. One of the Indians became obtrusively friendly, inviting him into his lodge. A sympathetic Indian woman, who suspected that McNeal might be killed for the blanket he had around him, ran screaming for help. Clark, who was not far away, sent some men to the village to investigate. McNeal had escaped from the lodge, and was found hastily retreating, more surprised than alarmed. Clark named the neighboring creek McNeal's Folly (now called the Nehalem River).

Many Indian girls visited the fort, but the captains urged their men to avoid them, particularly those who were selling their "indulgencies." Lewis and Clark feared venereal disease, which was rife among the Indians. Contacts between the natives and maritime traders had spread various ailments among the natives and had also caused a general cultural decline. The men saw a red-haired, freckled-faced Indian boy whose father, probably a sailor long gone, had refused to let his mother flatten the boy's head—a common practice among some of the coastal Indians. One of the Indian girls had "J. Bowman" tattooed on her arm.

Game was short during the winter. The elk in the region were wary, and unfavorable weather constantly interfered with hunting. Among a group of expert riflemen Drewyer was the only hunter who brought in elk meat regularly. Their only beverage, Lewis remarked sadly, was "pure water."

Sacajawea, for whom the winter was equally hard, had saved a small piece of bread made from real flour—not native roots—which she had been keeping for her baby. She gave it to Captain Clark, who ate it with relish, even though, as he wrote, "it unfortunately got wet."

The captains took advantage of the lull in activities to write reports and catalogue the Indian subtribes around— dozens of them with—to the explorers—unpronounceable names.[2] Clark finished his maps. Lewis classified trees, shrubs, ferns, fish, reptiles, and birds. In the journal entries for this month are many observations of Indian dress and tribal life. The men made moccasins. In one way or another everyone marked time, waiting to start for home. Their

[2] One example will suffice: the "Cookoooose" (whose spelling would be somewhat improved by a hyphen: "Cookoo-oose"). It was later decided by etymologists that *coos* in one of the dialects meant "lake," "lagoon," or "inland bay."

primary mission had been fulfilled. They had found a route to the Pacific.

The men traded almost daily with the Indians, but they were nearly out of trade goods. In March they admitted having only enough to tie up in two handkerchiefs. For a little amusement some wore Indian hats made by the Clatsops— tall hats woven from cedar bark and bear grass with small brims "of about two inches and a high crown widening upward." Some preferred a neighboring tribe's conical hats, which had no brim and were held on the head by a string under the chin. At one time hats were bought for the whole party.

As spring drew near, game grew even scarcer.[3] Hunters had to go so far from camp that only with great effort could they haul back the game they managed to shoot.

Tobacco gave out. The men, thirty of whom either chewed or smoked tobacco, had to fall back on crab-tree bark for chewing and the inner bark of the red willow for smoking. There was general sickness. Willard cut his leg with a hatchet, Gibson and Bratton were so ill that they could do no work. Bratton was suffering from a back ailment. He did not recover until the men were on the homeward trail.

The main purpose in camping so near the coast had been to find a sailing vessel that might take the party home by

[3] Some historians have suggested that the men could have made an effort to kill seals. The only seal meat they ate was given to them by the Indians. According to Shoshoni stories, Sacajawea thought the seals were a strange race of human beings. When she tried to "talk" to them, they slipped away into the water.

water. President Jefferson, for some reason—perhaps wishing not to stir up the Spanish government—sent no ships to meet the explorers. The Indians told of trading vessels that had been seen along the coast but failed to mention the brig *Lydia*, commanded by Captain Samuel Hill, which was sailing along the coast of Oregon and Washington through parts of 1805 and 1806. In fact, the vessel was in the estuary of the Columbia for at least a month, and Captain Hill had taken a small boat one hundred miles upriver before Lewis and Clark arrived. The *Lydia* was standing offshore in November, but fog probably prevented those on board from seeing the campfires.

Thus Lewis and Clark had to return home overland. A plan to leave a few men on the Pacific Coast was considered and abandoned. All the men wondered whether they would make it back, particularly those who had been ill during the winter.

As March wore on, there was a bustle of preparation around Fort Clatsop. Damaged canoes were repaired; Lewis sacrificed his fancy gold-laced uniform coat in exchange for another canoe; the guns were overhauled by Shields; 440 pounds of lead and powder were packed.

By March 15 the captains were getting spring fever. They noted on that day that the sorrel had put forth some leaves and the birds were singing "very agreeably."[4] On March 22 they turned Fort Clatsop over to Chief Coboway, and on

[4] Taken from "Remarks," notes appended to their daily weather reports, or "meteorological register." The notes were reprinted for the first time by Elliott Coues in *A History of the Expedition Under the Command of Captains Lewis and Clark*, III, 1293–94.

the next day the Lewis and Clark Expedition set out east-ward.[5] Sacajawea and her family accompanied them.

[5] Chief Coboway, who lived until about 1825, used Fort Clatsop as a fall and winter hunting lodge for ten or fifteen years. The fort was still standing when the Canadian explorer Alexander Henry visited it in 1831. In 1836, John Kirk Townsend, the ornithologist, found the logs still sound but the roof gone. By about 1850 only two cabins and some ruins were left. It has since been rebuilt and is now a national memorial.

The Walla Wallas

13

IT was raining when the Corps of Discovery left Fort Clatsop. No matter—they were accustomed to rain by this time (Gass commented that there were only six entirely clear days between November 5 and March 25). March 24 was clear after a rain, but the next day there was a heavy rainfall with thunder and lightning and more rain.

Paddling along among the Seal Islands, where the channel narrows near present-day Cathlamet, Washington, they took the wrong channel, but a Cathlamet Indian pursued them and directed them to the right channel. Then he embarrassed them by claiming that one of their canoes, which they had taken from the Clatsops in reprisal for a theft, was his. The captains gave him an elk skin for it.

They discovered a large river, emptying into the Columbia from the south, about where Portland now stands, and the captains added it to their map. It was the Willamette, which had been hidden from their view by small islands as they went downriver the previous fall.

Until the expedition reached the Walla Wallas, they found the various tribes along the river sullen—not outwardly warlike, but uncooperative, perhaps because food was so scarce. Lewis had to resort to a demonstration of magic to trade with recalcitrant Indians for wapatoos. Unnoticed, he tossed an artillery fuse ("a port fire match") into an Indian campfire. The brilliant flame terrified them. Lewis then showed them his compass. Impressed and fearful, the Indians, to appease the wrath of the gods who seemed to be helping the captain, agreed to trade.

Thefts were a nuisance. The Indians went so far as to steal Scannon, who had faithfully served the explorers as a sentry. Lewis, who did not propose to let Scannon end his days in an Indian kettle, sent a rescue party to recover him.

The upriver trip in canoes was not an easy one. As soon as Indians with horses were encountered, trading began. By now the captains had almost nothing to trade. However, Clark treated the Indians for aches and pains, inflamed eyes, and other complaints in exchange for horses. Clark's "eye water" was especially in demand.[1] He complained on April 18 that one of his woman patients was a "sulky bitch," but he treated her anyway for back pains, since her husband, a chief, had some horses to trade.

As the men acquired horses, they discarded the canoes (one had already been lost in rapids). If the Indians would not trade horses for canoes, the boats were chopped up for firewood.

On April 27, Lewis and Clark revisited Yellepit, the friendly chief whom they had met the year before. Clark gave Yellepit his sword in exchange for an "elegant white horse." (A sword bearing the name Clark was found near Cathlamet, Washington, in 1904.)

Sick and injured Walla Wallas gathered in the explorers' camp. One had a broken arm that taxed Clark's skill as a physician. He undauntedly applied splints, and he treated others for colds, sprains, and rheumatism. The Walla Wallas were friendly and sociable, a welcome change from the hostile tribes between the ocean and the mouth of the Walla Walla River. The captains agreed to festivities, with square dancing and violin music. The next day the party was ferried across the river in canoes to resume travel on the south side of the Columbia. There they said good-by to one of their favorite Indian tribes and headed overland for the Snake (Lewis) River. At the Touchet River they found adequate firewood and game.

The men now had enough horses to journey cross-country. Charbonneau, not only the worst waterman of the expedi-

[1] A solution containing sugar of lead (lead acetate) and/or white vitriol (zinc sulphate).

tion but also a poor horseman, twice delayed the party by losing his horse. Sometimes Indian families would join them, breaking their line of march and slowing them down. But since the Indians were friendly and were trying to be helpful, they were allowed to remain.

As they moved up the Pataha Valley on May 1, the captains were astounded to be overtaken by three young Walla Walla braves, who returned a steel trap that had been overlooked on departure. "Hospitable, honest and sincere," was the praise given these Indians in the journals.

Among the Walla Wallas was a woman prisoner of the Shoshoni tribe. Although she belonged to a different group of Shoshonis, Sacajawea was able to communicate with her. "We were able to explain ourselves to the Indians, and answer all their inquiries with respect to ourselves and the object of our journey. Our conversation inspired them with much confidence."

Gradually Nez Percé Indians began to filter into camp. They too were friendly. On May 11, in order to address a number of Nez Percé chiefs, Lewis and Clark called in their battery of interpreters. The Nez Percés also had a Shoshoni prisoner. The captains gave their message, one sentence at a time, to a Frenchman of their party, who repeated it in French to Charbonneau. Charbonneau, who spoke broken English, relayed the message in Hidatsa to Sacajawea, who translated it into Shoshoni for the prisoner. By this roundabout method the captains communicated with the Nez Percés.

The Blue Mountains of northern Oregon were now in sight. The captains devoted some space in their journals to a description of the local hills in the spring:

We now find, for the first time since leaving Rock fort [The Dalles] an abundance of firewood. The growth consists of cottonwood, birch, crimson haw, red and sweet willow, chokecherry, yellow currants, gooseberry, the honeysuckle with a white berry, rosebushes, sevenbark and sumac, together with the corn grass and rushes.

Food was better too:

We were soon supplied by Drewyer with a beaver and an otter, of which we took only a part of the beaver and gave the rest to the Indians. The otter is a favorite food, though much inferior, at least in our estimation, to the dog, which they will not eat.

The men saw deer, curlews, cranes, ducks, and prairie larks along the way, but no herds of buffaloes or elk, so plentiful along the Missouri River. The expedition camped for a night at a site between what later would be the towns of Prescott and Waitsburg, Washington.

The Nez Percés

14

DURING May and part of June the Lewis and Clark Expedition traveled through Nez Percé country. They camped for some time on the South Fork of the Clearwater (in what is now Idaho County, Idaho), departing on June 10. No name is recorded for this stopping place, but it could well have been called Camp Chopunnish (near present-day Kamiah, Idaho).

Sacajawea continued to gather roots and to contribute substantially to the company's food supply. Lewis makes a journal entry under the date May 16: "Our sick men are much better today. Sahcargarweah gathered a quantity of the roots of a species of fennel, which we found very agreeable food. The flavor of the root is not unlike annis seed." On May 18 Clark noted that Sacajawea was gathering "year-pah" (yampa) roots, which could be eaten fresh, roasted, boiled, or dried and were "generally between the size of a quill and that of a man's finger, and about the length of the latter."

Game was easier to find but not plentiful until June; then bear meat and venison replaced the flesh of horses and dogs. The weather had improved somewhat, but every rain in the valleys meant snow on the heights. The Indians warned Lewis not to attempt the passage of the Bitterroots until June.

The captains continued to regard the Nez Percés as the most amiable and gentle Indians with whom they had associated. Indifferent to trinkets and baubles, the Nez Percés prized such useful items as knives, kettles, blankets, and awls.

Clark's medical practice grew much larger than he could handle. He did the best he could with the remedies at his disposal. It was not unusual for him to treat forty sick or injured Indians in one day. He remarked that, in any event, he did not give them anything that would hurt them. His eye water and liniments and laxatives must have been effective, for his reputation spread. "The extent of our medical fame is not a little troublesome," he lamented.

One of Clark's most worrisome patients was one of his

own men, Bratton, whose back was still so painful that he could scarcely sit up. For him the captains finally prescribed an Indian treatment—a sweat bath. The men dug a four-foot-deep pit, built a fire in it, and heated stones. The hot stones were placed in an enclosure, and water was poured on the stones. Bratton sat in the steam imbibing large quantities of horsemint tea. Periodically he was plunged into cold water and then returned to his steamroom. Finally he was wrapped in blankets. He began to improve the next day and soon recovered fully. After this success the captains gave an elderly chief, Tom-a-tap-po, who had suffered from partial paralysis for three years, the same treatment, and he too soon began to show improvement.

The most serious medical emergency at this time was the illness of Sacajawea's baby. Little Pomp, who had shared all the hardships of the journey, was now about fifteen months old. Both Pomp and his mother had seemed to be indestructible, but now he was suffering from a swollen neck and throat.

The captains poulticed his neck with wild onions and then tried a salve of resin, beeswax, and bear's oil. By May 25 the little boy was better.

During May the captains were busy rounding up the horses they had left with the Nez Percés the year before. They learned that three of the chiefs, Twisted Hair, Broken Arm, and Cut Nose, had quarreled over the care of the horses. All of them apparently anticipated rewards. Because of the quarrel the horses had been scattered during the winter. They were eventually rounded up, except for two that the Shoshoni guides of the year before had taken. The captains did not complain about it, since the guides had received no pay. Part of the cache of gear and supplies had been destroyed, but the chiefs had saved most of the saddles.

Mishaps were frequent. To get supplies for the mountain crossing, Charbonneau and LePage were sent out with meager trading goods to visit an Indian village. These two Frenchmen may have known how to deal with Indians, but they were inept with horses. They managed to let their packhorse fall into the river, lost some of their goods, and soaked the rest. Shannon, Collins, and Potts, also on a trading mission, upset their canoe and lost it, along with some of their clothing and blankets—a serious loss. Potts, unable to swim, barely escaped drowning.

One day a number of Nez Percé chiefs assembled at camp, probably for medicines and treatments. The captains decided that it was an opportune time to deliver one of their well-rehearsed orations. At least seven main chiefs and several subchiefs were present. Clark set out to tell the Indians all about the United States, the Great White Father, and the white men's desire for peace and trade with their Indian brothers.

The chain of interpreters again went into action. The message was passed from the captains to one of the more articulate Frenchmen, to Charbonneau, to Sacajawea, to the Shoshoni captive. He communicated the message to the assembled Indians. They seemed to understand. The principal chief harangued his men, urging them to agree to follow the advice of the white men, chiefly to keep peace. While the Indians debated this, a big meal of mush was being prepared in the kettles, and at the conclusion of his oration the chief instructed all those who wished to ratify the proceedings to join them in eating. The rest could abstain. Clark commented with dry humor: "There was not a dissenting voice on this great national question, but all swallowed their objections, if any they had, very cheerfully with their mush." For their co-operative attitude the chiefs received some medals.

On June 10 the expedition took to the trail again, going first to Quamash Flats, just west of Weippe Prairie (northwest of the present town of Weippe). Lewis wrote on that day: "At 11 a.m. we set out with the party, each man being well mounted, and a light load on a second horse; besides which we have several supernumerary horses, in case of accident or want of provision. We therefore feel ourselves perfectly equipped for the mountains."[1]

1 From June 10 to 16, 1806, the Lewis and Clark party hunted in the area of Weippe Prairie. The camas plants were in bloom, as well as violets, honeysuckle, huckleberry, and white maple. The fields of camas were described as appearing, from a short distance, like "lakes of fine clear water."

Recrossing the Bitterroot Mountains

15

FIVE days were spent preparing for the mountain crossing. The men were in high spirits. They had enough surplus energy to engage in foot races, pitch quoits, and play "prisoner's base." Nothing seemed to dismay them, not even the prospect of wading into the mountain snows or failing to shoot enough game for the trip. They dried what meat they had, packed their baggage the night before departure, and were ready to start.

On June 15 the expedition commenced a swift, forced march eastward over the Bitterroots. They intended to take the same high "buffalo trail" that they had followed on the western trip and cross the mountains in five days—no more, because that was as long as the horses could go without forage.

By June 17 they had climbed into the high ridges of the mountains, and there they bogged down. Lewis reported: "We found ourselves enveloped in snow from 12 to 15 feet in depth, even on the south side of the mountain. . . . Winter now presented itself in all its rigors; the air was keen and cold, no vestige of vegetation was to be seen, and our hands and feet were benumbed." They were forced to backtrack, returning to Hungry Creek. After one camp they retreated to Weippe Prairie.[1] Drewyer and Shannon were sent back to try to find Nez Percés who would guide them over the mountains as far as Traveler's Rest Creek (near present-day Missoula, Montana).

Mishaps of the next day were described by Gass:

We proceed on [while waiting for a guide] with four men in front to cut some bushes out of the path; but did not go very far till one of the men [Potts] cut himself badly with a large knife; when we had to halt and bind up his wound. We went again forward, and in crossing the creek the horse of one of our men [Colter] fell with him, threw him off, hurt his leg and lost his blanket.

[1] Ordway liked the prairie and commented that he wished he could stay there. "Plenty of strawberries," he wrote.

These were the critical days of the journey home. The men were unable to proceed. No guides had been found. Two horses were lost, and a search party had set out to look for them. Two men were injured. There was almost nothing to eat. Cruzatte found some mushrooms, which the ravenous men ate without knowing whether they were poisonous. Fortunately, they were edible.

Another of their horses was injured on June 21, as the backtrack continued. About then two Indians rode up, leading four extra horses. They were setting out to cross the mountains in the direction Lewis and Clark wanted to go. They were persuaded to wait for the full party to reassemble. Drewyer and Shannon soon returned with three more Indians.

The next day one of the Indian guides fell behind, declaring that he was ill and unable to travel. The captains interpreted this to mean that he was not eager to cross the mountains. A companion turned back with him. As it turned out, the guide really was ill. He and his companion caught up with the party a few days later, the sick man so poorly clad—in only an elk-skin shirt and moccasins—that the captains gave him a buffalo robe.

On June 26 the men faced the mountain crossing again, finding that the snow banks had shrunk slightly and that there were a few patches of grass for the horses. But it was bear grass, which the horses disliked so much that they seemed to prefer to starve. By June 28 the party had plodded twenty-eight miles without taking the loads from the horses. A rest stop was made, and lunch was "bear's oil with some boiled roots." They pitched camp at midday because of the extreme fatigue of both men and beasts.

The mountains looked bleak and impassable to Lewis and Clark, but the native guides knew what they were doing. Lewis wrote that they "traverse this trackless region with a kind of instinctive sagacity; they never hesitate, they are never embarrassed; and so undeviating is their step, that wherever the snow had disappeared for even a hundred paces, we find the summer road."

The Corps of Discovery came out of the Bitterroot Mountains on June 29. Lewis reported: "We continued along the ridge which we have been following . . . till at the end of five miles it terminated; and bidding adieu to the snows in which we have been imprisoned, we descended to the main branch of the Kooskooskee." The party went wearily down Lolo Creek to Lolo Hot Springs, Montana. The short but torturous mountain crossing was over. The horses could feed on grass at last, and for the first time in two years the men had a hot bath at the springs. That night they reached Traveler's Rest Creek.

The Party Divides

16

WHILE at Traveler's Rest in the Bitterroot Valley, Lewis and Clark made the decision to divide the party for the remainder of the return trip. Lewis wanted to explore the sources of the Marias River. Clark would take the most direct route he could find—shorter, it was hoped, than the looping one followed on the way west—to the Beaverhead River, where the expedition had cached boats. Both parties would then subdivide. Lewis' party would divide at Great Falls, which Lewis would reach overland; Clark's at the Beaverhead. Lewis would leave some men at Great Falls. Clark would send some of his men downriver to Great Falls to help with the portage. Clark would then proceed to the Yellowstone River overland, sending from that point another group by land with the horses to the junction of the Yellowstone and the Missouri, while he took the river route. All would reassemble at the mouth of the Yellowstone (near the North Dakota line).

If all went well, Lewis' route would take him northeast to Great Falls, thence north to the Marias; Clark's route, southeast to the Beaverhead, thence east to the Yellowstone. Charbonneau and Sacajawea would accompany Clark. Both routes would be dangerous, and everyone knew that this separation might be a final one. Lewis wrote that he hoped it would be "only momentary."

Nez Percé guides were persuaded to travel for a day or two with Lewis and his party. Then they departed, a little fearful of the "Pahkees" (their enemies, the Hidatsas), not far from present-day Missoula. Lewis' route followed Hellgate Canyon, then up the Blackfoot River and north across the Dearborn River to the Sun River, which he followed east to the Missouri at present-day Great Falls. To follow this route, the party had to cross a low pass on the Continental Divide, which has since been known as Lewis and Clark Pass, although Clark never crossed it. Lewis' party would reach Great Falls on July 13.

Meanwhile, Clark's party followed the main fork of the Bitterroot River and on July 5 camped at Ross's Hole (near where the expedition had first met the Flatheads). Following an old buffalo trail, they found another pass across the Continental Divide (Gibbon's Pass), which would permit them to go directly southeast to the Beaverhead. Sacajawea recognized the plain; her tribe had gone there often to dig camas roots.

On July 7, Clark's men found some hot springs. Two of the men, experimenting, found it possible to cook meat in the bubbling spring waters. The next day they reached the junction of Horse Prairie Creek and the Beaverhead, the point at which they had left the Beaverhead the year before. They found the cache of canoes and supplies in good condition. The men were delighted to find their prized supply of chewing tobacco intact. Clark remarked with amusement that the tobacco chewers, who had been out of tobacco for half a year, scarcely gave themselves time to take the saddles from their horses before they were off for the cache.

Pausing for some preparations and repairs, Clark sent Sergeant Pryor and some of the men overland toward Three Forks with the horses, while he ventured onto the river downstream with the rest. Both groups would meet again at Three Forks on July 13.

When Lewis and his party arrived at Great Falls on July 13, they found game plentiful. It was mating season for the buffaloes, and great herds of them were milling around. The bellowing of the bulls created a constant roar, upsetting the horses, who were unused to buffaloes. Both parties complained of ever-increasing swarms of mosquitoes. Clark thought that the deer were thin because of the insects, and the horses had to be held within a circle of smoking campfires for protection. Sacajawea's son especially suffered from mosquito bites. Clark's party also had to endure cold, windy weather. Freezing rain fell and then turned to ice; snow appeared imminent—in July. The journals report three-quarters of an inch of ice on standing water on the night of July 10. Still there were mosquitoes aplenty until dark.

Sacajawea was familiar with this part of the country, and she was able to assure Clark that they were on the right route and could cross the Continental Divide by continuing in their present direction.

After reaching Three Forks, Ordway and nine others loaded baggage into six canoes and then started down the Missouri to join Lewis at Great Falls. Clark and the rest of his party (now consisting of Pryor, Shields, Shannon, Bratton, Labiche, Windsor, Hall, Gibson, Charbonneau, Sacajawea, Pomp, and York) started eastward overland, looking for the Yellowstone River.

Lewis Explores the Marias River

17

BETWEEN July 13 and July 17, Lewis and his men, camped at Great Falls, prepared to divide again, one group to go north and explore the Marias River, the other to proceed downstream on the Missouri. Some of Clark's men were expected momentarily from Three Forks. Clark himself and the rest of his group were moving eastward, cross-country, with a band of forty-nine horses and one colt.

Clark's journey toward the passes of the Rocky Mountains, through which they must find a route, provided the background for one of the controversies of the return journey: Did Sacajawea now guide the expedition? And did she pick the best route?

The party set out eastward on July 13 but journeyed only four miles that day, halting with lame horses on the north bank of the Gallatin River. By July 15, however, they had traveled nine miles beyond the top ridges of the Continental Divide and had reached the Yellowstone. Sacajawea recommended the pass now called Bozeman Pass.

Clark's exact route from Three Forks to the Yellowstone is relatively unimportant; he could have made the crossing through any of three different passes in the region. C. S. Kingston declared that "it was solely on [Sacajawea's] advice that Clark decided to go to the Yellowstone by the Bozeman Pass route. But he did not know when the party started for Bozeman Pass that there was a wide expanse of swamp ground which must be crossed . . . an intolerable route!"[1] Kingston thought that she should have suggested Flathead Pass.

Biddle's edition of the journals agrees that Sacajawea recommended Bozeman Pass:

The squaw now assured Captain Clark that the large road from Medicine (Sun) River to the gap they were seeking crossed the upper part of this plain. He therefore proceeded four miles up the plain and reached the main channel of the

[1] "Sacajawea as Guide," *Pacific Northwest Quarterly*, Vol. XXXV (January, 1944). Kingston was indulging in hairsplitting. Sacajawea recommended a trail followed by her tribe. More than that could hardly be expected of her.

river (West Gallatin), which is still navigable for canoes, though much divided and dammed up by multitudes of beaver. Having forded this river, they passed through a little skirt of cottonwood to a low open plain, where they dined.[2]

According to Biddle, Sacajawea added some information. She told the captains that, a few years before, buffaloes had been numerous not only in that region but even as far as the sources of the Jefferson River.

As Clark looked eastward on July 13, he saw the Bridger Range and, southward, the Gallatin Range. The East Gallatin River emerged from between the ranges, south of Bridger Peak and north of Mount Ellis. The gap "to the southward" was the one Sacajawea recommended. Clark took her advice and later wrote, "The Indian woman . . . has been of great service to me as a pilot through this country."

Coues commented that Clark "very sensibly followed the advice of the remarkable woman, who never failed to rise to the occasion, even when it was mountains high. He accordingly makes the Bozeman Pass . . . and strikes the Yellowstone at its nearest point, by the most direct route."[3] Sacajawea's route enabled the Clark party to proceed forty-

[2] Coues (ed.), *A History of the Expedition Under the Command of Captains Lewis and Clark*, III, 1132–33.

[3] Clark and his party did do some floundering around in the marshes of the West Gallatin River. Everything considered, however, they made remarkable time between Three Forks and the Yellowstone. Their route was later the one selected for the Northern Pacific Railroad and also for the main highway. Part of it was a buffalo road. Coues pointed out: "The other gap . . . would have taken [Clark] over Flathead Pass of the Bridger range, and so to Flathead creek and other upper tributaries of Shields' river, a good deal north of his best route." Coues (ed.), *A History of the Expedition*, III, 1132.

eight miles between July 13 and July 15, marshes and rivers notwithstanding. They were now in the Yellowstone Valley, not far from the present town of Livingston, Montana.[4]

Clark expected to find some Crow Indians in the valley. He did not actually see them, but he was soon convinced that they were nearby, for horses began to disappear nightly. Canoe travel would have been easier than overland travel, but no trees suitable for large canoes were to be found.

Accidents occurred. Charbonneau, always inept with horses, fell with his mount while pursuing a buffalo. The Frenchman was shaken up and bruised. Gibson, trying to mount a skittish horse, fell on a sharp charred snag that penetrated his thigh two inches, making it necessary to carry him on a litter. On July 21 the men found some timber and began building canoes. It was none too soon, for the next morning twenty-four horses were missing. By then travel by water seemed preferable.

On the morning of the twenty-fourth, near present Billings, Montana, Pryor, Shannon, and Windsor set out to take the remaining horses overland to Fort Mandan, while Clark and the rest of the men pushed off in loaded canoes down the Yellowstone. The canoes were so small that they were lashed in pairs. Both parties made camp together that night, but Pryor reported difficulty driving a band of horses with only three riders. The horses, trained by Indians, insisted on chasing buffaloes. Clark added Hall to Pryor's party, and since Hall was just about naked, he was given a spare shirt, leggings, and moccasins. By now all the men were ragged and insufficiently clothed.

Meanwhile, Lewis and his men were having considerably

4 Bernard De Voto (ed.), *The Journals of Lewis and Clark*, 449.

more excitement. They too had lost some of their horses, and they almost lost McNeal, whose horse plunged into brush at the White Bear Island camp near Great Falls and found himself face-to-face with a grizzly bear. The horse wheeled and threw McNeal practically at the bear's feet. As the huge beast rose on his hind legs, McNeal swung his rifle and struck the bear over the head, breaking the weapon. As the stunned beast clasped his head, McNeal climbed the nearest tree and stayed there until the angry bear finally stalked away.[5]

On July 17, while Clark and his men were looking for timber along the Yellowstone, Lewis left Sergeant Gass and five others at Great Falls to portage supplies from the cache, with instructions to wait for the group coming downriver from Three Forks and then meet Lewis at the mouth of the Marias River. Lewis took with him only Drewyer and Joseph and Reuben Fields to investigate the sources of the river on the north.

For a week the Lewis party continued up the Marias after intersecting it overland and then turned back toward the Missouri. As Drewyer walked along the river bottom—the rest on higher ground—Lewis saw a group of horses about a mile away. He studied them through his glass and made out a small band of Indians standing silently, watching Drewyer. He was sure that they were Blackfeet—always harbingers of trouble—and they had horses.

[5] Sergeant Patrick Gass's published journals, which contained drawings of expedition episodes executed by an artist with only a vague conception of conditions, illustrates McNeal's plight with a sketch that shows a bear looking more like Lewis' Newfoundland than a grizzly, and McNeal sitting placidly on a tree limb wearing a high-crowned hat and a long-tailed coat.

Thus was the stage set for Lewis' only important error in judgment during the expedition—and a fight, by morning, which resulted in the certain death of one Indian and probably two. The date was July 26; the place, on the south fork of the Marias River, not far from present Cutbank, Montana.

A Skirmish with the Indians

18

LEWIS thought that he counted thirty horses or more as he studied the group of Indians on the hill through his glass. He determined that perhaps eight of the horses were saddled, indicating a larger party of Indians than he had at first supposed. He decided upon a friendly approach—especially since the Indians had spotted Drewyer. For their part, the Indians, who gave evidence of alarm and indecision on seeing the white men, rode toward Lewis and his two companions. At a distance of one hundred yards Lewis dismounted to meet one of the Indians who was approaching while the others waited.

Now began Lewis' most critical effort at diplomacy. He asked by signs whether the Indians were Hidatsas. The Indians indicated that they were Blackfeet. Lewis inquired whether any among the party were chiefs. They replied that three were chiefs. Not likely, Lewis thought. He gave away a flag, a medal, and a handkerchief. The two parties eyed each other for a while. The white men wondered nervously whether there were any more Blackfeet. The Indians appeared equally ill at ease, doubtlessly wondering whether another party of white men would appear.

Finally Lewis proposed that both groups camp together, probably because he wanted to keep an eye on the Indians. The Indians agreed. Both groups sought to convince each other that they were parts of large forces. Men were coming up the Missouri to the mouth of the Marias, Lewis informed the Indians solemnly. The Indians told him that two large bands of Blackfeet were nearby, one camped on the main branch of the Marias.

After having made the mistake of suggesting that they camp together, Lewis and his men compounded the error by not remaining alert. They smoked with the Indians until a late hour, and then Lewis ordered Joseph Fields to stand guard. Everything about camp was quiet until sunrise, when the Indians arose and crowded around a fire that Fields had built. He had carelessly left his rifle near his brother, who was still sleeping. One of the Indians slipped behind them, seizing both the brothers' guns. Two other Indians seized the rifles belonging to Lewis and Drewyer, and one started to run away. Lewis heard Drewyer yell, "Damn you, let go of my gun!"

A furor erupted. The Fields brothers chased the nearest Indian, overtook him, and wrestled with him for the gun. Drewyer battled with the Indian who had taken his gun, and Lewis, awakened by the commotion, drew his pistol and ran after another Indian.

An Indian was stabbed in the scuffle with the Fields brothers. The Blackfoot ran a little distance and fell dead. Lewis overtook the Indian he was chasing and ordered him to drop the gun or be shot. As the Fields brothers came running up, Lewis called out to them to hold their fire and try to recover the horses, which other Indians were running off.

Lewis again set out with his pistol after the Blackfoot who had stolen his gun and another Indian, who was attempting to steal the horses still in camp. As Lewis later wrote:

I called to them as I had done several times before that I would shoot them if they did not give me my horse and raised my gun, one of them jumped behind a rock and spoke to the other who turned around and stopped at the distance of 30 steps from me and I shot him through the belly, he fell to his knees and on his wright elbow from which position he partly raised himself and fired at me, and turning himself about crawled in behind a rock which was a few feet from him. he overshot me, being bearheaded I felt the wind of his bullet very distinctly.

Lewis' shot probably was fatal to the Indian, but the journals do not verify his death.[1]

[1] Weapons were lethal enough in those days, but it took from

Drewyer soon returned from his pursuit of the Indians, and the Fields brothers returned shortly with four horses. In their flight the Blackfeet had left some of their belongings, including bows and arrows, which Lewis burned in the campfire. The men hastily saddled, taking one of their own horses and four of the Indians'. They lost no time heading for the mouth of the Marias. This was the longest almost continuous trail ride in the history of American expeditions. The men jolted for sixty-three miles the first day, stopping briefly at the Tanzy River to allow the horses a short rest, and then pushed on another seventeen miles. By 2:00 A.M. the next morning they had ridden almost one hundred miles. At last, feeling reasonably safe from pursuit by friends of the dead and wounded Blackfeet, they dismounted and slept.

The next morning the men were so stiff that they could scarcely move. Nevertheless they pressed on toward the Missouri. Near the hills along the banks of the river they heard gunshots. Was a fight already in progress? The shots proved to be those of Sergeant Ordway and nine men who on July 19 had joined Gass and those already at Great Falls after coming downriver from Three Forks.

Lewis and his men could have crossed the Marias River and put more distance between themselves and the Indians, but Lewis had decided to go to the mouth of the river, the agreed meeting place. His decision was based partly on his conviction that the Blackfeet would pick the junction as the

---

twenty to thirty seconds to fire a second shot. Lewis did not have his powder with him and thus could fire only once with his pistol.

point to intercept them.[2] "I told [the men] that we owed much for the safety of our friends and that we must risk our lives on this occasion," the captain explained in his journal. Later he reported, "We had the unspeakable satisfaction of seeing our canoes coming down." The two parties saluted each other by gunfire, and the men in the canoes paddled to shore. All warmly shook hands.

[2] Many years later a Blackfoot in the group that had had the skirmish with Lewis said that the Indians were just as frightened as the white men and rode off in another direction to put as many miles between them and the white men as possible.

The Mouth of the Yellowstone

19

ON July 24, the day before Lewis and his friends met the Indians near the Marias River, Clark and his water party had started down the Yellowstone River and were making good time with the help of a swift current. They saw a now-famous rock "in an extensive bottom on the right, 250 paces from the shore." They estimated that it was about two hundred feet high. On the rock Indians had carved figures of animals and other objects. Clark named it Pompey's Pillar. After climbing it and looking over the countryside, Clark descended and cut his name and the day, month, and year on the face. His signature is still visible on the rock, protected by a grillwork—another of the few remaining physical signs of the expedition. A town named for the landmark stands nearby.

The party camped near the mouth of the Bighorn River on July 26, and on the next day, when Lewis and his men were involved in the shooting incident with the Indians, Clark's party made more than eighty miles downriver—practically flying, in comparison with the slow trip up the Missouri the year before. By July 30 they had reached the mouth of the Powder River.

From this point they began to see more buffaloes and some grizzly bears. Clark wrote: "The buffalo now appear in vast numbers. A herd happened to be on their way across the river. Such was the magnitude of these animals, that, though the river, including an island over which they passed, was a mile wide, the herd stretched, as thickly as they could swim, from one side to the other." The shaggy swimming animals caused an hour's delay.

Clark's party reached the mouth of the Yellowstone on August 3, and although this was the point where they were to meet Lewis, the mosquitoes were so troublesome in the windless heat that they decided to go farther downriver. Clark wrote a note to Lewis, fastened it to a pole at the confluence of the rivers, and then moved on to another camping place (which proved to be even more mosquito-infested). By now little Pomp's face was badly swollen,

Clark noted. Clark went out to shoot bighorns, but insects clouded the barrel of his rifle, making his gunsights useless.

The storms and rain of the next two days were welcome, for the mosquitoes disappeared temporarily. On August 8, to everyone's surprise, Sergeant Pryor, with Shannon, Hall, and Windsor, came paddling downriver in skin boats. At a point near Pompey's Pillar they had made themselves circular skin canoes like the Mandans' bull boats and had been happy to find the frail vessels ideal for skimming downstream. Unfortunately, Pryor had removed most of Clark's note to Lewis at the junction of the Yellowstone and the Missouri, but at least he and his men had learned from it where Captain Clark was, and they continued paddling downstream until they caught up with him.

Sacajawea continued gathering roots and berries for the party. Clark reported that she gathered "a large well-flavored gooseberry, of a rich crimson color, and a deep purple berry of a species of currant common on the river as low as the Mandans, and called by the engagees Indian currant."

Meanwhile, Lewis and his small party, exhausted by their headlong ride from the Blackfeet, had been joined by the men who had come downriver from Great Falls. They turned the horses loose and again set out on the Missouri from the mouth of the Marias River. They had hoped that the red pirogue they had cached there would still be usable, but it had rotted.

Sergeant Ordway's party, which had left the mouth of the Madison River on the thirteenth, had departed from Great Falls on the twenty-seventh in the white pirogue and five canoes. Sergeant Gass and Willard had set out from that point by land, taking horses with them. All the groups met at the mouth of the Marias and were headed down the Missouri, making rapid progress. The river was high, and game was plentiful. The Lewis party reached the junction of the Musselshell on August 1 and the mouth of the Milk River on August 4. The same hot weather that Clark complained of also oppressed Lewis' party on the Missouri. Later they were pelted by the same rains. At times the wind was so high that it was not safe to put loaded canoes into the water. Nevertheless, they reached the mouth of the Yellowstone on August 7, where Lewis was a bit puzzled to find a scrap of paper on a pole, with only his name on it, in Clark's handwriting.

Pressing on to catch Clark's waiting crew, on August 11 they saw some elk on a sandbar thick with willows. Lewis and Cruzatte landed to try to shoot one. Lewis, who had experienced most of the close escapes of the expedition, was now to experience one more. Both he and Cruzatte shot at an elk and then separated in the underbrush to find it. Just as Lewis was preparing to shoot again, he heard a rifle crack, and a ball struck him squarely in the backside. Cruzatte, who was nearsighted, had mistaken Lewis for an elk and had shot his captain. The ball passed through the left side of Lewis' buttocks, grazed the right one, and dropped into his breeches. Fortunately, it struck no bone or artery.

Lewis yelled, "Damn you, you have shot me!" Then, when Cruzatte did not answer, he wondered whether the shot might have come from Indians. Lewis hobbled back to the pirogue, fearing that Indians might attack at any time. Cruzatte finally appeared, apologizing profusely for his stupidity.

The bleeding wound was dressed, and Lewis lay down in the boat, ignominiously put out of action just before he and Clark were reunited. After the next day, August 12, Lewis, because of the pain of his wound, discontinued his journal.

Down to St. Louis

20

LEWIS' party caught up with Clark on August 12. Clark, looking across the water as shots were fired in salute, at first could not see the captain. Lewis' wound was so painful that he could barely move, and he had to stay in the pirogue, even at night.

The next day, aided by a stiff breeze, the reunited explorers made eighty-six miles downriver and felt that they were practically in home country as they drew near Fort Mandan. On August 14 they reached an encampment of Hidatsas.

Captain Clark called the Hidatsa chiefs together and addressed them through the interpreter Jussome, whom Drewyer had been sent to find at the Mandan villages. Clark wanted one of the chiefs to visit the Great White Father in Washington, but the chiefs were full of excuses— afraid to pass through the land of the Sioux. Despite Lewis' and Clark's arguments and hopes for peace, intertribal wars had continued. Charbonneau, visiting with the Indians, reported that the Hidatsas had been fighting both the Shoshonis and the Arikaras and had all but gone to war with the Mandans in an argument over a woman.

Clark went to see Le Borgne, "the great chief of all the Minnetarees" [Hidatsas], who at the time was living at one of the Mandan villages, and invited him to visit the Great Father, but he too said that the Sioux would prevent him from going.[1] Finally She-he-ke (Big White) of the Mandans agreed to go to Washington, provided he could take along his wife and son and also Jussome, his wife, and two children.

Colter, the only member of the expedition who appeared not to be eager to go home, asked permission to accompany two white traders named Dickson and Hancock into beaver country. Lewis and Clark gave him permission to leave.

[1] It is unlikely that Le Borgne was afraid of the Sioux or anyone else. He was a fearsome chief, a one-eyed giant with a violent temper. He was probably using the Sioux as an excuse for avoiding the journey to Washington.

At Fort Mandan the explorers bade farewell to Charbon-neau and Sacajawea. On August 17, Clark wrote:

Settled with Touisant Charbono for his services as an enterpreter the price of a horse and Lodge (leather tent) purchased of him for public Service in all amounting to 500$ 33 1/3 cents. derected two of the largest of the Canoes be fastened together with poles tied across them So as to make them Study [steady] for the purpose of Conveying the Indians and enterpreter and their families.

we were visited by all the principal Chiefs of the Mene-tarras to take their leave of us at 2 oClock we left our en-campment after takeing leave of Colter who also Set out up river in company with Messrs. Dickson and Hancock. we also took our leave of T. Chabono, his Snake Indian wife and their child who had accompanied us on our rout to the pacific ocean in the capacity of interpreter. . . . T. Chabono wished much to accompany us in the said Capacity if we could have provailed (upon) the Menetarre Chiefs to decend the river with us to the U. States, but as none of those Chiefs of whoes language he was Conversent would accompany us, his services were no longer of use to the U. States and he was therefore discharged and paid up. we offered to convey him down to Illinois if he chose to go, He declined proceeding on at present, observing that he had no acquaintance or prospects of makeing a liveing below, and must continue to live in the way that he had done. I offered to take his little son a butifull promising child who is 19 months old to which they both himself & wife wer willing provided the child had been weened. they observed that in one year the boy would be sufficiently old to leave his mother & he would then take him to me if I would be so friendly as to raise the child for him in such a manner as I thought proper, to which I agreed &c.

Sacajawea received no pay, but Clark apparently expected to make it up to her later.

After much weeping by She-he-ke's friends and relatives, the stocky, prematurely gray Mandan chief and his entourage boarded the canoes, and the Lewis and Clark party glided downriver.[2] The swivel gun had been given to Le Borgne, who fired it and then took it with great ceremony to his village.

Lewis spent an uncomfortable two weeks nursing his wound. On the twenty-third, Clark noted that Lewis was recovering rapidly. But on the twenty-seventh Lewis did too much walking, and on the thirtieth Clark was a little more cautious in reporting that "Captain Lewis is mending slowly." Finally on September 9 he reported: "My worthy friend, Capt. Lewis, has entirely recovered. His wounds are healed up, and he can walk and even run nearly as well as he ever could."

All the members of the party except for Chief She-he-ke were happy as they floated down the Missouri toward St. Louis. The chief and his family were already weary of the journey. They soon met traders on the Missouri. A party

[2] The Mandan chief made a longer visit in the United States than anyone bargained for. In 1807, Clark arranged to send him back upriver with an escort under Nathaniel Pryor, but the Arikaras were hostile. One of their chiefs had died on such a visit. A fight developed along the river: Shannon, the former member of the expedition, suffered a bad leg wound, and his leg was later amputated. Jussome, the interpreter friend of the Mandan chief, was also injured in this encounter. She-he-ke refused to accompany the party overland to the Mandan villages. It was not until 1809 that he was finally delivered back to his people. His sojourn among the whites had given She-he-ke, already too talkative, a great deal to relate, which his tribesmen found hard to believe. The Mandans branded him a liar.

136

of Frenchmen, manning a boat owned by Auguste Chouteau, gave the returning explorers a gallon of whisky—only a sip for each person, but deeply appreciated—their only drink of "spirits" since July 4, 1805. A few days later traders LaCroy, Aiten, and Chouteau, commanding three boats, gave the thirsty men all the whisky they could drink. That evening they were very hilarious, singing songs until midnight.

Making fifty or more miles daily, by September 20 the Corps of Discovery was nearing St. Louis. The men saw cows grazing along the banks of the river. At sundown the town of La Charette came into view. People rushed to the riverbank to see the returning explorers; they had long since been given up for lost. Nothing had been heard from them since they left the Mandans more than a year and a half before.

The last half of September, 1806, was unusually warm. Clark had reported September 8 as the hottest day of the year, but September 16 was still warmer. Clark described it as "emencely worm." Thirty-two hard-rowing, bearded men in dugout canoes, their clothes ragged and their skin burned brown, were coming down the river, resting momentarily to fire volleys of rifle shots. They had traveled eight thousand miles.

Clark's notation on September 23 reads: "Descended to the Mississippi and down that river to St. Louis at which place we arrived at 12 o'clock. We suffered the party to fire off their pieces as a salute to the town." His shortest notation was made on September 26: "A fine morning. We commenced writing, etc."

The Expedition Ends

21

THE Lewis and Clark Expedition had ended. A postrider waited at Cahokia, Illinois, to take a letter to President Jefferson. As the news spread across the country, the importance of the Louisiana Purchase was realized. It had been proved that there was a land-and-water route to the Pacific Ocean.

The members of the expedition separated and went their

own ways, never again to reassemble. Lewis and Clark each received 1,600 acres of land from the government, and each of the other members were allotted 320 acres, though few settled on them. All were to receive double pay for the time they spent on the journey, about $166 for each man and $1,228 for each captain.

Meriwether Lewis was appointed governor of Louisiana Territory; William Clark was made brigadier general of the Louisiana militia. In 1809, while en route from St. Louis to Washington, Lewis died under mysterious circumstances in a dingy little roadside hostelry in frontier Tennessee. He may have been murdered; he may have taken his own life. At the time of his death Lewis was on his way to explain to Jefferson some of his problems as territorial governor.

Clark rejected the opportunity to succeed Lewis as governor of Louisiana Territory, but he later became governor of Missouri Territory and superintendent of Indian Affairs at St. Louis. He was universally admired and respected, had great personal influence among the Indians, and was responsible for thirty Indian treaties. After a long and useful life, Clark died in 1838 at the age of sixty-eight.

As for the other members of the famous expedition, some returned to the wilderness. John Colter opened the route to Jackson Hole, Wyoming. Some became farmers; others fought in the War of 1812.[1] Shannon became a judge; Willard settled in California; Drewyer and Potts lost their lives to the Indians; and some simply disappeared from history. One, Paddy Gass, lived to be almost one hundred years old. York died of cholera a few years after the expedition.

---

[1] Among them Bratton and Gass. Bratton married and fathered ten children. Gass married at sixty and fathered seven children.

But what of Sacajawea, Charbonneau, and little Baptiste? For a while they remained at the Mandan villages after the expedition went downriver to St. Louis. Then, on August 20, Captain Clark, writing from the Arikara village below future Fort Manuel, sent a letter to Charbonneau:

Charbono:

Sir: Your present situation with the Indians gives me some concern—I wish now I had advised you to come on with me to the Illinois where it would most probably be in my power to put you in some way to do something for yourself. . . . You may have been a long time with me and have conducted yourself in such a manner as to gain my friendship; your woman, who accompanied you that long and dangerous and fatiguing route to the Pacific Ocian and back, deserved a greater reward for her attention and service on that route than we had in our power to give her at the Mandans. As to your little son (my boy Pomp) you well know my fondness for him and my anxiety to take and raise him as my own child.[2] I once more tell you if you will bring your son, Baptiest, to me, I will educate him and treat him as my own child—I do not forget the promise which I made to you and shall now repeat them that you may be certain— Charbono, if you wish to live with the white people, and will come to me, I will give you a piece of land and furnish you with horses, cows and hogs—if you wish to visit your friends in Montrall, I will let you have a horse, and your family shall be taken care of until your return—If you wish to return as an interpreter for the Menetarras when the troops come up to form the establishment, you will be with me ready and I will procure you the place—or if you wish to

[2] Clark's affection for Baptiste is apparent throughout his journal.

return to trade with the Indians and will leave your little son Pomp with me, I will assist you with merchandise for that purpose . . . and become myself concerned with you in trade on a small scale, that is to say not exceeding a pirogue load at one time. If you are disposed to accept either of my offers to you, and will bring down your son, your femme Janey[3] had best come along with you to take care of the boy until I get him. Let me advise you to keep your bill of exchange and what furs and peltries you have in possession and get as much more as you can, and get as many robes, and big horn and cabbra skins as you can collect in the course of this winter. And take them down to St. Louis as early as possible. . . . Inquire of the governor of that place for a letter which I shall leave with him. . . . I shall inform you what you had best do with your furs, peltries and robes, etc. . . . When you get to St. Louis write a letter to me by the post and let me know your situation—If you do not intend to go down either this fall or in the spring, write a letter to me by the first opportunity and inform me what you intend to do that I may know if I may expect you or not. If you ever intend to come down, this fall or the next spring will be the best time—this fall would be best if you could get down before winter. I shall be found either in St. Louis or in Clarksville at the falls of the Ohio.

Wishing you and your family great success, and with anxious expectations of seeing my little dancing boy, Baptiste, I shall remain your friend.

WILLIAM CLARK

Keep this letter and let not more than one or two persons see it, and when you write to me seal your letter. I think you best not determine which of my offers to accept until you

[3] Clark's nickname for Sacajawea.

see me. Come prepared to accept . . . which you may choose after you get down.[4]

Thus Clark gave the family an opportunity to go to St. Louis and enter the white man's world. Charbonneau accepted the offer and took Pomp and Sacajawea to St. Louis. Later, when Charbonneau decided to return to the Upper Missouri, Sacajawea went with him, leaving her son in St. Louis.

[4] For ease of reading, Clark's spelling (except for names) has been corrected.

Sacajawea — What Was She Like?

22

MUCH of Sacajawea's life is shrouded in mystery. The year and a half she spent with the Lewis and Clark Expedition is the only documented period of her life. During that time she served the United States faithfully and without pay, although it is doubtful that she comprehended the significance of the expedition.

Of her life before and after the expedition much less is

known. She was born into a tribe of Northern Shoshonis somewhere in Idaho's Lemhi Valley. Her early days were spent wandering with her people through the mountains of Idaho and Montana. Kidnapped by a party of raiding Hidatsas, she was taken east to the Great Plains, hundreds of miles from her home.

The girl must have longed for her home and family, although, except for the moving story of her reunion with Cameahwait, there is no record that she ever gave expression to her longing.

Charbonneau, a rough, aging, unchivalrous fur trader, either bought Sacajawea from the Hidatsas or won her in a gambling game and took her for his wife. When she was only sixteen, Sacajawea lay in pain on buffalo robes in a fort in the wilderness, with only bearded men around—and perhaps an interpreter's wife—and in a difficult delivery gave birth to a baby boy. Less than two months later she set out for the Pacific with Lewis and Clark with her baby on her back.

Picture a slight, active Indian girl, with the black hair and copper skin of most Shoshonis of her time. This small Indian girl endured discomfort and semistarvation and survived a year and a half of rigorous travel, much of it afoot, caring for a baby, accepting her share of difficult tasks.

When the expedition started, Sacajawea was probably freshly clothed in fringed deerskin. As time went on and conditions of travel worsened, she no doubt wore any garments she could patch together. Even in the hardest times, however, she probably found ways to decorate her clothing. Like most girls, Sacajawea liked beads. But she gave her blue-beaded belt to the captains when they needed it for trade. She probably carried her belongings and those of her baby in a parfleche, a buffalo skin cut into a pattern and folded over, laced, decorated, and perhaps painted.

Any appraisal of Sacajawea must depend on the fragments of reference to her in the diaries and journals of the Lewis and Clark Expedition, plus statements made by explorers who said they knew her—though they did not refer to her by name—a few years afterward.

The first characteristic of Sacajawea's described in the journals was compassion. She tried to protect another Indian woman from an angry husband at Fort Mandan. Soon after the expedition was under way, she demonstrated coolness in emergency and courage in the face of danger. She won the admiration of the captains on the day the pirogue nearly capsized. Whenever the Indian girl appears in the journals, the reference is generally to her usefulness. No fault was ever found with her. She was alert and industrious, a busy berry and root gatherer. Sometimes she showed the men Indian ways of cooking and of eking out a scanty meal.

As the only woman on the expedition, it is certain that she helped nurse the sick and injured, mended clothes and moccasins, and scraped and tanned skins—at the same time caring for her tiny son.

The members of the party were half-starved throughout much of the mountain travel. Little surprise that after Sacajawea's one recorded sick spell she ate too much. Queasy stomachs were frequent on the expedition. There was too much to eat or too little, the weather was too hot or too cold, and the water supply in the plains was muddy.

Lewis, alone among the diarists in trying to describe

Sacajawea's nature, once wrote that she possessed a "folly or philosophy" that enabled her to accept life as she found it. Almost without fail she radiated cheerfulness. Captain Clark called her uncomplaining. This trait must have been conspicuous to have elicited such a comment.

Sacajawea was also impulsively generous, a girl who gave a lump of hoarded sugar to her brother and a precious piece of bread to Captain Clark.

On only one occasion, on November 14, 1805, during the interminably rainy stay at the mouth of the Columbia River, did Sacajawea display pique. Captain Clark wrote, "Squar displeased with me," but he failed to explain why.

It is obvious that even before the party left the Mandan villages, the captains had concluded that Sacajawea was going to be useful to them on the journey. She became much more useful than they expected.

No historian is likely to assert now that the Indian girl was indispensable to the party. The members might have survived without her root digging and berry picking, her cooking, sewing, and nursing. They might have succeeded in obtaining horses from her tribe without her help. Lewis might have forestalled the Shoshonis' departure to hunt buffalo without her warning. Yet there can be no question that her presence eased the way. As mentioned earlier, it may be that Sacajawea's greatest contribution was simply her presence. Tradition has it that the Nez Percé contemplated killing the straggling party as it crossed the Bitterroots on the way west but that an Indian girl who had been befriended by white men dissuaded her tribesmen by asking, "Why do these white men have an Indian girl with a baby along? Surely this cannot be a war party."

Historians disagree about how much help Sacajawea actually was in guiding the Clark party eastward through Bozeman Pass. No doubt Clark could have experimented with other routes, but he might have been later—much later—reaching the Yellowstone with horses whose hooves were already worn to the quick.

There were instances when Sacajawea strengthened morale. She reassured them, when the expedition was all but lost while trying to find a western Rocky Mountain crossing, "In that direction you are sure to find my tribe."

How did Sacajawea fare as the only woman member of a boisterous expedition made up almost entirely of bachelors? Indian girls were generally accorded little respect. It was customary to think of the girls as chattels. Charbonneau had the typical fur trader's careless attitude toward Indian womanhood. Not noted for refinement, delicacy, patience, or kindness—who among the fur traders was?—he may have quarreled with her frequently and may have mistreated her. He did indeed strike her in one recorded instance when Captain Clark intervened.

Fur traders married Indian girls because they needed them. It is not accurate to say that the women provided only sex. Wives were indispensable to the mountain men, and many wives were well treated. Some of the roughest characters of the plains and mountains were inconsolable when they lost their wives, and most of them loved their half-blood children. It was the pinnacle of many Indian girls' ambitions to marry a fur trader.

It is overstating the case to claim, as romanticizers tend to do, that Sacajawea suffered for a cause. Any reader of the journals of the expedition is impressed by her enjoyment of

life. She had spunk and energy and endurance. Outdoor life
was the only life she knew. It must be remembered that she
was a Shoshoni, and Shoshonis came from a cold and in-
hospitable homeland in the Rockies. They were inured to
hardship and lack of food and were seldom bowed by mis-
fortune. The Shoshonis were often gay and carefree under
conditions that white men found all but intolerable. It is
probable that Sacajawea's life as a Hidatsa captive was not
entirely unhappy, either. Probably she was permitted to
enjoy some of the freedom of Hidatsa girls below the age
of marriage.[1]

After she joined the expedition, the fact that Sacajawea
was married and a mother doubtless restrained any amorous
inclinations on the men's part. The journals indicate that
Charbonneau and Sacajawea were permitted a certain
amount of privacy; the interpreters and their wives shared
a tent with the captains. As for Pomp, he was a favorite. As
soon as he learned to toddle, the men played with him,
danced around with him, or dandled him on their knees.

Thus it is likely that Sacajawea enjoyed a reasonably
happy life with the Lewis and Clark party. In fact, her lot
may have been an improvement over that of many another

[1] George Catlin told of crossing the Missouri River with two others
in a bull boat, assisted by laughing, screaming Hidatsa maidens. He
wrote: "We were soon surrounded by a dozen or more beautiful girls
twelve to eighteen years of age. . . . They all swam in a bold and
graceful manner, as confidently as so many otters or beavers; and with
their long black hair floating on the water, whilst their faces were
glowing with jokes and fun, which they were cracking about us and
which we could not understand." Harold McCracken, *George Catlin
and the Old Frontier*, 112.

Indian girl. She was in her most active years and should be pictured that way—not as a prematurely aging woman bowed down with burdens.

As for the often-repeated suggestion that Sacajawea had a romantic attachment for Captain Clark, it is indeed possible that she did. No doubt he was a much more attractive man than Charbonneau. But Lewis and Clark had to maintain a certain posture before their men. They were emissaries of the President and were under the constant observation of their men.

Many of the tribes were afflicted with venereal disease, the scourge left by coastal traders, for which the Indians had no cure. Both Lewis and Clark cautioned their men against relations with Indian women suspected of being diseased. Apparently the warning went unheeded. Clark mentioned the use of mercury in treating his men.

Though the captains evidently avoided any personal contact with Indian women, they observed them and often described them in their journals. Indian women were ranked from "handsome" to "disgusting." The captains thought that the Mandan girls were exceptionally good-looking. Some of the coastal tribes had pleasant enough faces but tied their ankles and feet so tightly as to restrict circulation and cause misshapen legs. Some of them had elongated heads, which were not attractive to white men. Others painted themselves too liberally, smeared their hair with bear oil, or wore costumes that appeared ludicrous to white men.

The captains did not think that in general Indian women were particularly chaste. Among the exceptions were the

Shoshonis and the Nez Percés. Of the Shoshonis, Lewis writes: "Some of their women appear to be held more sacred than in any nation we have seen."

To the end of her days Sacajawea continued to be held in unusually high esteem. Two contemporary writers spoke well of her. Henry Brackenridge, the author-explorer, who wrote that he met her on a boat going upriver from St. Louis in 1811, thought her "a good creature of mild and gentle disposition." John Luttig, the clerk at Fort Manuel, who tersely reported her death there, called her "the best woman at the fort."

At Fort Manuel

23

SACAJAWEA'S life after she parted company with the Lewis and Clark Expedition has been the subject of controversy among scholars and mythmakers. It appears almost certain, however, that in 1806, some months after the expedition ended, Sacajawea, Charbonneau, and Baptiste, at Clark's invitation, went down the Missouri to St. Louis, where they hoped to make a life for themselves. Grace

FORT MANUEL, 1812

Raymond Hebard, who wrote a popular account of Sacajawea's life, believed that Charbonneau took both of his Shoshoni wives and two sons with him.[1] Leaving his family there, the interpreter accepted an offer to trap for a fur company on the rivers of the Southwest.

Miss Hebard identified the second boy as Baptiste's half-brother, Toussaint. Later historians believe that there was probably only one boy, Baptiste called by two different names.

On October 30, 1810, Charbonneau purchased from Cap-

[1] Grace Raymond Hebard, *Sacajawea: Guide of the Lewis and Clark Expedition*.

tain Clark, who was then Indian agent for Louisiana Territory, a tract of land on the Missouri River, in Saint
Ferdinand Township, near St. Louis. In the spring of 1811,
Charbonneau sold the land back to Clark for one hundred
dollars, a transaction recorded on March 26, 1811. Charbonneau must have decided that he did not want to farm
and was homesick for the plains, the fur traders, and his
Indian friends. About the time he sold his tract of land,
Charbonneau bought fifty pounds of "biscuit" (the hard-
tack of those days), apparently anticipating employment
with Henry Brackenridge's party on the boat going upriver.

An entry in Brackenridge's journals reads:

We have on board a Frenchman named Charbonet, with
his wife, an Indian woman of the Snake nation, both of
whom accompanied Lewis and Clark to the Pacific, and
were of great service. The woman, a good creature, of mild
and gentle disposition, was greatly attached to the whites,
whose manners and airs she tries to imitate; but she had
become sickly and longed to revisit her native country; her
husband also, who had spent many years amongst the Indians, was become weary of a civilized life.[2]

By providing Charbonneau with an extra wife and son in
St. Louis, Miss Hebard was able to argue that Brackenridge
mistakenly identified the Indian woman with Charbonneau
as Sacajawea. She insisted that the woman mentioned by
Brackenridge was not Sacajawea but another Shoshoni wife,
the mother of the second Indian boy and that Baptiste, only
six years old, was too young to be left in St. Louis without a
mother. Thus, Miss Hebard claimed, "Sacajawea . . . re-

[2] Henry M. Brackenridge, *Journal of a Voyage Up the Missouri
River in 1811.*

mained to care for her son and also to have oversight of the other boy, Toussaint."

John Bradbury, the English naturalist, confirmed Brackenridge's statement that Charbonneau and his wife went upriver in April, 1811. In view of the fact that Miss Hebard offered no proof for her version of events, there seems no reason to question Brackenridge's identification.

Two expeditions set out from St. Louis in the spring of 1811: Brackenridge with Manuel Lisa, the fur baron; Bradbury with the Astorians under Wilson Price Hunt. These men headed competitive parties, both after the fur trade. The Astorians left the Missouri River and reached the Pacific Coast by an overland route, suffering many hardships along the way. Bradbury left the party when it started overland and returned to St. Louis. Charbonneau traveled as far as Mandan country, and made various villages in the region his headquarters for many years. He also joined the Lisa expedition of 1812, although it is not clear at what point or whether Sacajawea accompanied him on a trip he made to St. Louis in 1812. Only Charbonneau's name appears on the list of *engagés* hired for the 1812 trip.[3]

Lisa's party was to build Fort Manuel (named for him) just below the North Dakota border in South Dakota, on the banks of the Missouri. John C. Luttig, a former Baltimore and St. Louis businessman, went along and became clerk for Lisa at Fort Manuel. Luttig kept a daily journal of activities at the fort until it was abandoned in 1813.

His journal, which is a primary source of information about the troubles with the British and Indians in the

[3] John C. Luttig, *Journal of a Fur Trading Expedition on the Upper Missouri, 1812–1813* (ed. by Stella M. Drumm), 158.

region in 1812, is also our main evidence that Charbonneau spent some time at the fort. Luttig mentioned Charbonneau several times, generally in a derogatory manner.

Luttig began his journal with the departure of the boat from St. Louis. He reported that eighty-seven persons were aboard and that the boat was accompanied by two barges loaded with goods, including the first domesticated animals other than horses to be taken to the Upper Missouri.

The fort was constructed on the present line between North and South Dakota, and its completion was cele-brated on November 19. The festivities included a dance, attended by all the ladies of the fort. During its short life, the fort was the site of almost frenzied activity. People came on foot, on horseback, by boat. Indians of many tribes, traders, trappers, and hunting parties came on all kinds of missions. There were women, children, dogs, and horses in profusion. Drunken brawls, horse stealing, lost livestock, unwelcome campers, domestic quarrels, accusations, and suspicion abounded. Amid the general furor there was a busy traffic in goods of various kinds.

Luttig's daily log indicates that confusion—even pande-monium—prevailed much of the time. He must have been a busy man, and that may explain the terse, sometimes hur-ried entries in his journal:

August 13, 1812: At 10 P.M. 60 Rees composing a War party arrived. they requested something to eat....

August 14: ... last night about 40 Indians camped with us. they were gathering Cherries and other fruits about the Country.

August 26: Grey Eyes (Ree Chief) arrived with 100 men from a war tour. They had not killed or even seen an enemy.

In the evening a larger party passed by with Two Scalps. . . .

September 11: Mr. Lewis, two engages and the trappers for the little Horn, in all 18 Men [arrived]. At noon a Sioux Chief arrived. . . .

September 17: The Men who went to gett the Horses came back and told the sad news that 5 Indians, supposing Grosventers, had mounted the horses in their sight and rode them off.

September 21: . . . the Sioux after having taken a little mixed whisky, pretended to be drunk, and cut Capers about like mad men. . . .

October 15: A Band of Chajennes, about 12 Lodges arrived, their chief named Lessaroco. They had plenty of Women & Children and a great Number of Dogs. . . .

November 14: . . . the Saunie Sioux had arrived with about 150 Lodges at the Rees. . . . a band of Chajennes were camped about 5 miles above the fort. . . .

Luttig's entries reporting deaths at the fort were also brief. On December 20, 1812, he wrote: "This evening the wife of Charbonneau, a Snake squaw, died of a putrid fever. She was a good and the best woman in the fort, aged about 25 years. She left a fine infant girl." Luttig did not record the woman's name—perhaps because he, like the diarists of the Lewis and Clark Expedition, had trouble spelling it. Perhaps he did not even know it.

The fort itself did not survive long. The Indians were becoming hostile. On February 5, 1813, a young Hidatsa hunter was shot and killed just outside the gates. "The Sioux!" Luttig exclaimed. On February 22 one of the *engagés*, Archambeau, was hauling hay on a sled. As he approached the opposite shore of the river, he was shot by Indians. "They took the scalp and cut him nearly to pieces,"

Luttig reported. The fort's swivel guns could not be trained on the four or five hundred Indians Luttig claimed were poised across the river. Most of the men who had come upriver with Lisa were scattered for many miles, trapping or trading, and the fort was not well protected. Women and children outnumbered defenders. On February 26, Luttig complained that those remaining in the fort "are like Prisoners in Deserts to expect every moment our fate." His journal ends on March 5: "Snowstorm last night and continued snowing all this Day...."

Within a few days the fort was abandoned, and the occupants scattered. Luttig took with him the baby girl whom he called Sacajawea's Lizette. Luttig, a man of sympathetic feelings, felt a responsibility toward the child, even though he was not overly fond of her father. Fort Manuel was evidently burned by the Indians. Luttig arrived in St. Louis in June, 1813, and in August applied to the court to be appointed guardian for Lizette, as well as for "Toussaint," a boy about ten years old. In the court record the name Luttig was subsequently crossed out and William Clark's substituted. Luttig died in 1815.

Charbonneau, who was undoubtedly away from Fort Manuel when it was abandoned, can be traced in later diaries and journals of the western explorations and occasionally through official records. Although he survived until his eighties, he was never reunited with his children. He evidently did not return to St. Louis after 1816, when he left on a trading trip for Auguste Chouteau.

Despite Luttig's journal record of Sacajawea's death at Fort Manuel, in Shoshoni oral tradition Sacajawea rejoined her tribe years later on the reservation. Baptiste, who was often called Toussaint, can be followed until 1866, the probable year of his death, although in Shoshoni tradition he too reappeared with his tribe and lived in Wyoming with his aged mother and Bazil, the son of her dead sister, whom she had adopted in 1805. By the latter account Baptiste lived until 1885, Bazil until 1886. Both briefly outlived their mother, who died in 1884. The Shoshoni tradition will be discussed in the chapters that follow.

There is no record of what became of Lizette. On April 23, 1843, the daughter of one Joseph Vertifeuille and Elizabeth Carboneau was baptized at Westport, Missouri. The little girl's name was Victoire. It is at least possible that Victoire's mother, Elizabeth (née "Carboneau"), was Sacajawea's daughter.

Toussaint Charbonneau

24

THE fairest appraisal of the fur trader and interpreter
Toussaint Charbonneau was that of O. D. Wheeler, who
wrote: "It has been rather the fashion of latter-day writers
and critics to sneer at and decry the old interpreter. [But]
. . . Charbonneau was, after all, a man of fairly commend-
able traits considering his environments."[1]

[1] O. D. Wheeler, *The Trail of Lewis and Clark*, 1804–1806.

It would be difficult to visualize Toussaint Charbonneau in "civilization." He was born in or near Montreal, Canada, about 1759. From the time he was in his twenties, he was making his fortune among the fur traders and Indians on the frontiers. In 1793 and 1794 he was employed by the Northwest Fur Company at Pine Fort, on the Assiniboine River. Several years later he went to North Dakota. He was staying with the Hidatsas near the Knife River when Lewis and Clark met him.

He could be pictured as short, swarthy, and bearded, talkative, perhaps boastful. Some said that he was high-strung and had a quick temper. The Indians regarded him with some amusement, and the nicknames they gave him, such as "Chief of the Little Village" and "Great Horse from Afar," were bestowed in mockery, but not necessarily in antagonism. The fact that he lived among the Indians until he was past eighty is proof enough that he was their friend. Unfortunately, he was a constant pursuer of Indian girls; when we first meet him in the journals of the fur traders, he is in the bad graces of an Indian girl's mother.

Charbonneau appealed to the western explorers and mountain men because he knew his trade. When his ability to translate Indian words failed him, he could interpret sign language. Those who sometimes called him a villain or a knave were generally his competitors. He had his failings. On the Lewis and Clark Expedition he proved to be accident-prone, a timorous waterman, a poor horseman, and at times slow-witted. He certainly did less for the party than his wife, Sacajawea, did. Yet, as the oldest member of the group, he endured hardships that exhausted men much younger than he. Although he was seldom praised by Lewis or Clark, he was sometimes commended for his on-the-trail cookery and his emergency meals. Coues was inclined to believe that Charbonneau was a "minus function" and described him as a "poor specimen, consisting chiefly of a tongue to wag in a mouth to fill." But Lewis and Clark referred to him as their "friend" and noted that he performed his duties satisfactorily, although he had no "peculiar merit."

Other notable explorers and adventurers took advantage of his skills. Prince Paul of Württemberg employed him in 1823. He was favorably mentioned by General Henry Atkinson in 1825, by Major Stephen Kearny, also in 1825, and by Captain Reuben Holmes, who met him in 1833. (Holmes commented that Charbonneau never carried a rifle—that a knife was his only weapon.)

In the 1830's, James Kipp, a Canadian with the American Fur Company, frequently employed Charbonneau as an interpreter. In the books of the Mandan Agency, it is recorded that from November 30, 1828, to September 30, 1834, Charbonneau was paid $2,437.32 for his services as an interpreter between the whites and the Mandans, Gros Ventres (Hidatsas), and Crows. He had his detractors, however. William Laidlaw, in a letter to Kipp from Fort Pierre, dated January 14, 1834, wrote: "I am much surprised at your taking old Charbonneau into favor after showing so much ingratitude upon all occasions."

Others were less critical. Prince Maximilian of Wied, a former Prussian army officer who traveled in the American West, met Charbonneau in 1843 and was favorably impressed by him. He expressed indebtedness to Charbonneau for many valuable accounts of the manners, morals, and habits of Indian tribes. Charbonneau was undoubtedly crude, but he was scarcely as inept as some writers have characterized him.

According to Stella M. Drumm: "Charbonneau had many friends among the traders, Indian agents and travelers of the West. In letter-books and manuscripts to be found among the archives of the Missouri Historical Society, as well as in many published narratives of travellers, are many favorable references to him."[2]

The old interpreter was durable. He was around Fort Clark and the Mandan villages through the years of cholera and smallpox (1835 to 1837), when he was apparently spared from either disease, although, according to the fort records, he lost still another Indian wife during the period.

All his life—into his eighties—he was marrying Indian girls. Typical of his experiences is one related by Chardon, the factor of Fort Clark, who wrote in his journals on October 22, 1834: "Charbonneau and his lady started for the Gros Ventres on a visit (or to tell you the truth) in quest of one of his runaway wives—for I must inform you he had two lively ones. Poor old man." Chardon also mentioned that in 1838, Charbonneau, at nearly eighty, married an Assiniboine girl of fourteen. He reported that the young men of the fort gave the couple a "splendid Charivaree." Of those years, Bernard De Voto wrote, Charbonneau was as "old as Rameses but active as ever."

In 1838, Charles Larpenteur and his fur traders met Charbonneau not far from Fort Clark. They said that the interpreter was wearing pants and a red flannel shirt. Evidently, despite his long years among the Indians, he never

[2] Luttig, *Journal of a Fur Trading Expedition*, 137.

adopted Indian dress. The last note that history took of Charbonneau was in 1839, when he appeared at the Office of Indian Affairs in St. Louis, tottering under the infirmities of eighty winters, to ask Joshua Pilcher, superintendent of Indian Affairs, for salary due him for services rendered the United States government. Apparently Charbonneau had been dismissed as interpreter after smallpox virtually wiped out the Mandan tribe in 1837, but the old man had continued to serve for some time, unaware of his dismissal. On August 26, 1839, Pilcher wrote to the Indian Department in Washington: "This man has been a faithful servant of the Government—though in a humble capacity. I . . . think it but right that he should be paid."

It may be assumed that the interpreter had had some narrow escapes during his lifetime on the plains (certainly he had had his share on the Lewis and Clark Expedition). The last documented one was revealed in a letter from Major David D. Mitchell to W. N. Fulkerson, Indian agent for the Mandans, dated June 10, 1836. Mitchell wrote that "old Charbonneau" had barely escaped death, "two balls having passed through his hat," when a Sioux shot at a Hidatsa boy in the interpreter's room at Fort Clark.

The date of Charbonneau's death and the site of his grave are unknown. Hebard says that he may have married a Ute woman and eventually died among the Ute Indians in Utah, but no Indian agency in Utah has a record of his death or burial.

Charbonneau's colorful life has been summed up as follows:

Toussaint Charbonneau: perhaps the first white man to

live in the Mandan-Minnataree towns, associated with the earliest traders at Pembina—Lewis and Clark, Sacajawea, Auguste Chouteau, Brackenridge, Luttig, Manuel Lisa, Jules de Mun, Long, Kearny, Prince Paul, Colonel Leavenworth, General Atkinson, Maximilian, John Jacob Astor, "the Liberator," Larpenteur, Pilcher—every name important on the Missouri prairies. The old Frenchman knew them all.

And just perhaps out there somewhere on those prairies where the buffalo bulls no longer stomp and roar, but where the long, lean coyote still cries across the snow—just perhaps, we say—the soul of old Charbonneau still wanders Missouri trails.[3]

[3] Gordon Speck, *Breeds and Half-Breeds,* 148.

Jean Baptiste Charbonneau

25

JEAN Baptiste Charbonneau, the son of Toussaint Charbonneau and Sacajawea, began his travels at the age of two months. He journeyed from the Mandan villages in North Dakota to the Pacific Ocean and back again with Lewis and Clark—by canoe, on his mother's back, on horseback, or in the arms of a bearded white explorer.

He accompanied his father and mother to St. Louis, probably in 1806, almost certainly before 1810. In 1811 his father, and apparently his mother too, left him there in the care of William Clark or someone designated by Clark. In 1813, John Luttig became the legal guardian of "Toussaint Charbonneau" and his sister, Lizette.

Several circumstances suggest that Toussaint was actually Baptiste. A son of Charbonneau, usually identifiable as Baptiste, can be traced with fur traders and explorers until 1846, the year of the Mexican War, and in California thereafter until 1866, when he set out on a trip to the Idaho or Montana gold fields and died on the way. No other son of Charbonneau's is mentioned in contemporary records. On the occasions when Toussaint (or "Tessou") is mentioned, the chances are that Baptiste was being given his father's name and that he was regarded as a "junior."

As late as 1820, Baptiste was being educated in St. Louis, for Clark's papers show sums for tuition paid during that year to both a Baptist minister and a Roman Catholic priest and other payments for school supplies, books, clothing, board, lodging, and laundry. The payments were made in behalf of "J. B. Charbonneau" or "Toussaint Charbonneau" (almost without doubt the same boy).[1]

In 1823, Prince Paul of Württemberg, a twenty-year-old explorer, was given permission to travel up the Missouri River. He met both Baptiste and old Charbonneau. In the prince's account of his travels, which was published in 1835,[2] he described his first meeting with Baptiste, near the mouth of the Kaw River, on June 21, 1823:

[1] American State Papers, 1820, Missouri Historical Society, St. Louis.
[2] *A Trip to North America*, Huntington Library, San Marino, Calif.

Here I found also a youth of sixteen,[3] whose mother was of the tribe of Sho-sho-ne, or Snake Indians, and who had accompanied the Messrs. Lewis and Clark to the Pacific ocean in the years 1804 to 1806 as interpretress. This Indian woman was married to the French interpreter of the expedition, Toussaint Charbonneau by name. Charbonneau rendered me service also, some time later in the same capacity, and Baptiste, his son (the youth of sixteen) of whom I made mention above, joined me on my return and followed me to Europe, and has remained with me ever since.

Prince Paul and Baptiste did not return to America until 1829. In that year Prince Paul received permission to make another trip into Indian country and traveled as far as the Mandan region. The journal of this expedition has never been found.

When he returned from Europe, Baptiste was well educated and could converse fluently in German, Spanish, French, and English. Despite his Continental education, on his return to America he apparently resumed life on the frontier. Up to 1846 western narratives mention him frequently and identify him clearly. Baptiste accompanied Prince Paul on the 1829–30 expedition. He was with the Robidoux Fur Brigade in 1830. In 1831 he may have been with Joseph Meek, who claimed that on his way from Powder River, Wyoming, to St. Louis he was accompanied by "a Frenchman, Cabenau."

W. A. Ferris, in his "Life in the Rocky Mountains," a memoir of his experiences in 1830–35, tells of an earlier experience, on the Lewis and Clark Expedition, with "Char-

[3] Baptiste was actually eighteen at the time.

bonneau, one of our men . . . the infant who, together with his mother, was saved from a sudden flood near the Falls of the Missouri." Nathaniel Wyeth mentioned Baptiste in his journal, saying that, after the Indians stole some horses, "Charbonneau pursued them on foot." Baptiste was also with Jim Bridger in 1832 and at the Green River traders' rendezvous in 1833. According to Walter S. Campbell, in *Kit Carson*, "Chabonard," Sacajawea's son, told Indian stories to Carson's company in 1839. In 1850, T. J. Farnham, in *Life, Adventures, and Travels in California*, mentioned meeting an educated Indian at Fort El Pueblo, five miles from Bent's Fort, in Colorado. The man was probably Baptiste.

According to E. Willard Smith, Charbonneau was with Vásquez and Sublette on the South Platte River in 1839. He mentioned two Indian traders and added: "One of them was a son of Captain Clark, the great Western traveler and companion of Lewis. He had received an education in Europe during seven years." Smith, who thought that Baptiste was Clark's son, spelled the trader's name "Shabenare." In 1842, Baptiste was in charge of a fur-trading party on the South Platte. In his journal of his expedition of 1842, John Charles Frémont mentioned "Chabonard's camp, on an island in the Platte." He said that the Frenchman was in the service of Bent and St. Vrain, and he praised his cooking ability.

A month or so later, Rufus B. Sage visited the men of the same party, who were waiting for high water to proceed downriver. He wrote: "The camp was under the direction of a half-breed, named Chabonard, who proved to be a gentleman of superior information."

In 1843 a party of more than eighty hunters on the Oregon Trail, led by Sir William Drummond Stewart, included one Baptiste Charbonneau, who was listed as a cart driver. In this group were also listed Captain Jefferson Kennerly Clark, a son of William Clark, and William Clark Kennerly, a nephew of Clark, for whom he was named.

Baptiste was apparently at Bent's Fort for a time. W. M. Boggs mentioned him in a chronicle covering the years 1844–45. Boggs wrote:

This Baptiste Charbenau, or half-breed son of the elder Charbenau that was employed by the Lewis and Clark expedition to the Pacific Ocean, had been educated to some extent; he wore his hair long so that it hung down to his shoulders. It is said that Charbenau was the best man on foot on the plains or in the Rocky Mountains.

Baptiste accompanied Lieutenant J. W. Abert on an exploring expedition down the Canadian River from Bent's Fort in 1845. Thomas Fitzpatrick, a mountain man with the party, praised the guide, "Mr. Charbonard," for his ability. Baptiste was included in George Frederick Ruxton's list of important fur traders in his book *Life in the Far West*. Ruxton described "Charbonar, a half-breed, . . . last in height, but first in every quality which constitutes excellence in a mountaineer."

In 1846–47, "Charbonneaux" accompanied Lieutenant Colonel Philip St. George Cooke and his troops through New Mexico to California. Cooke made a note in his journals that Baptiste could read and sign his name and was a skillful guide and hunter, like his mother before him. He could also speak Spanish. In Cooke's entry for November,

1846, he reported that "Charbonneaux" had encountered three grizzly bears "far up among the rocks" and killed one of them. Cooke gave his guide much credit for the success of his expedition to California, which traversed some of the most dangerous country in the Western world.

From these accounts one can construct a vivid picture of Baptiste: a short, dark, rugged man, intelligent and courageous, and a skilled guide, hunter, and mountaineer.

Baptiste apparently stayed in California. After the Mexican War he is said to have become alcalde of San Luis Rey. Later he moved to Placer County, where he lived until 1866. In that year he started for the gold fields of Montana and Idaho, contracted mountain fever, and died at Inskip's Ranch and Stage Station on Cow Creek, near the present town of Danner, Oregon.

On June 2, 1866, the *Owyhee Avalanche* of Ruby City, Idaho, reported his death. His death was also recorded in the *Placer Herald*, of Auburn, California, on July 7, and in the *Butte Record*, of Oroville, California, on July 14, 1860.

The Two Versions

26

IN the early years of the twentieth century Grace Raymond Hebard and Charles A. Eastman pieced together, with similar conclusions, the traditional Shoshoni account of Sacajawea's later life.[1] In the 1900's, Miss Hebard corresponded

[1] Grace Raymond Hebard was a teacher of history and political economy at the University of Wyoming, Laramie. She was especially interested in the Shoshoni tribe and devoted many years to research

with Mrs. Eva Emery Dye, who in 1902 had published a novel about Sacajawea, *Conquest*. Miss Hebard also corresponded with the Reverend John Roberts, an Episcopal missionary to the Shoshonis. In the 1920's the Indian Bureau asked Eastman to try to trace Sacajawea's life. In Miss Hebard's book about Sacajawea, published in 1932, she seems to have relied partly on Eastman's investigations.

Miss Hebard suggested that, when Charbonneau went to St. Louis in 1806, he took with him a new wife, Eagle, of the Hidatsa tribe. Sacajawea apparently made no objection to sharing her home. According to Miss Hebard and Eastman, Charbonneau later obtained employment with a fur company and took with him two wives, Eagle and Sacajawea, and two sons, Baptiste and "Toussaint," one or both of whom Clark had been educating. Both Miss Hebard and Eastman were convinced that there were two sons.

According to Miss Hebard, somewhere in western Oklahoma or Kansas the "polygamous old interpreter" took still another wife, a Ute woman, young and beautiful. Before long she and Sacajawea were quarreling over domestic matters. One day Charbonneau whipped Sacajawea, and she left him. She wandered from tribe to tribe, finally making her home with the Comanches, a branch of the same linguistic stock as that of the Shoshonis. In time Sacajawea mar-

---

on the life of Sacajawea. She died in 1936. Charles A. Eastman was born in 1858. His father was a full-blood Santee Sioux, and his mother was half Sioux. He held various posts with the Bureau of Indian Affairs. In 1903 he was sent into the Sioux region to establish a system of recording Indian surnames. In 1925 he made his report on Sacajawea to the commissioner of Indian Affairs. In his last years he was a lecturer and a homeopathic physician.

ried a Comanche named Jerk Meat and "lived harmoniously for a number of years, giving birth to five children." Later Jerk Meat was killed in battle, and Sacajawea began wandering again. The Comanches, not knowing her whereabouts, referred to her as Wadze-wipe (Lost Woman). Her Comanche son Ticannaf searched for her in vain among the Wichitas and Kiowas.

With her daughter, Yago-Wosier, this version continues, the Indian woman, no longer young and wishing to return to her tribe, followed the explorer John Charles Frémont from Comanche territory to Fort Bridger, in Wyoming, where the Lemhi branch of the Shoshonis was now living.

In July, 1843, at St. Vrain's Fort, Frémont wrote an account of a Shoshoni woman with his party:

A French engage at Lupton's fort in Colorado had been shot in the back on July 4th, and died during our absence to the Arkansas. The wife of the murdered man, an Indian woman of the Snake nation, desirous, like Naomi of old, to return to her people, requested and obtained permission to travel with my party to the neighborhood of the Bear river, where she expected to meet some of their villages. Happier than the Jewish widow, she carried with her two children, pretty little half-breeds, who added much to the liveliness of the camp. Her baggage was carried on five or six packhorses; and I gave her a small tent, for which I no longer had any use, as I had procured a lodge at the fort.

On July 18, near Ham's Fork of Black's Fork on the Green River, the Indian woman took leave of Frémont's expedition, expecting to find some of her people at Bridger's Fort, which had been established that year. She may have found some Shoshonis there, but after a time she left the fort and again wandered for a number of years, finally settling down permanently with her tribe sometime between 1850 and 1870.

Home at last with the Shoshonis, Sacajawea was reunited with her son, Baptiste, by Charbonneau, and her adopted son, Bazil. Her brother, Cameahwait, had been killed in battle about 1840. In 1862, Bazil suffered a crippling leg wound. He became known to the Indians as the lame sub-chief of Chief Washakie. In substance, the foregoing is Miss Hebard's reconstruction of the Indian version of Sacajawea's later life.

In the 1920's, Eastman undertook investigations which led him to the Shoshonis, Comanches, and Gros Ventres in Wyoming, Oklahoma, and North Dakota. He concluded that there was indeed a happy family reunion at Fort Bridger:

Bazil, the older son, . . . was exceptionally devoted to [Sacajawea]. It was in this family that she lived and died. There are many instances among the Indians where a nephew or step-son has been more devoted to the mother than the real son. This was the case in the relation of Bazil to this mother. It is the Ben Hur of the Indians. A most remarkable romantic life of any age.

To try to establish that Sacajawea lived among the Shoshonis, Miss Hebard interviewed the Indian woman's supposed descendants, as well as missionaries and agents. In 1905 the Reverend John Roberts, who in 1884 had officiated at last rites for the Indian woman (whom he sincerely believed to be Sacajawea), wrote:

I do not think Sacajawea's picture was ever taken, but

178

some of the old people tell me that one of her grand-daughters looks very like the heroine did in former days. . . . She understood French well. . . . The old lady was wonderfully active and intelligent, considering her age. She walked alone and was bright to the last.

The Indian agents credited this woman with much influence on her tribe until she reached old age. They said that she encouraged the Shoshonis to adopt white men's ways and learn to farm. According to them, she made her influence felt in the council at Fort Bridger in 1868, an unusual achievement for an Indian woman.

Fincelius G. Burnett, who went to the Shoshoni Indian Reservation in 1871 as agricultural agent ("boss farmer") to teach the Indians to farm, claimed to have known Sacajawea, her two sons, and many descendants. He said that she spoke both English and French and that she told him she had accompanied Lewis and Clark. She told of her capture by the Hidatsas, and she could describe "great fish" on the ocean shore and relate other incidents of the journey. Burnett described Sacajawea in old age as rather light in complexion, of medium size—"a very fine-looking woman and much thought of by the other Indians." She did not look her age: "You would have taken her son, Bazil, as the elder of the two."

James McAdams, a Shoshoni who attended Carlisle Indian School in Pennsylvania in 1881, told Miss Hebard that Porivo (the Shoshoni name for the woman who claimed to be Sacajawea) was his great-grandmother and Bazil his grandfather. He said that he had lived with his great-grandmother at one time and that she, Baptiste, and Bazil spoke French. Porivo had told him many times that she had "worked for the soldiers away off into the country clear to the big waters to the west." McAdams added that many persons had seen a gold-rimmed medal that Porivo cherished. The medal had Jefferson's likeness on it. He also said that his great-grandmother had given his grandfather Bazil some precious papers, which were placed in a leather wallet and, upon his death, were buried with him.

In 1926, Miss Hebard chanced to meet an old Indian woman who told her that she had met Porivo when she herself was only twelve years old. Porivo had told the girl's mother that she had traveled "with a large body of men over whom army officers were in charge, that the people became very hungry and killed some of their horses, and even dogs, for food."

In 1929, Tom Rivington, of Gering, Nebraska, wrote of this woman:

She was . . . not satisfied anywhere, and the stage companies helped to make her that way as they gave her free rides. . . . She told me she was as far south as the Gila river in Arizona. . . . She was over in California to see the Indians there, but said they were so poor, as the whites had taken all the country away from them, and she had been with the Nez Percé Indians in the state of Washington for several years. She had lived with different tribes up in Canada.

In 1871, James I. Patten became lay missionary to the Indians of the Wind River (Shoshoni) Reservation in Wyoming. There he saw and talked with the woman many were calling Sacajawea. He said that she spoke both English and French. In the late fall of 1874, Patten said, Bazil and Baptiste brought her to agency headquarters to be cared for while they were away on a buffalo hunt. They spoke of her as their mother. Patten said that during his long period of years on the reservation he daily saw Wadze-wipe, who was also called Lost Woman, Sacajawea, the Boat Pusher, Bah-ribo, and Water White-Man. She told him that she had accompanied Lewis and Clark on the expedition to the Pacific Ocean and that her son, Baptiste, was a "little papoose whom she carried on her back from the Mandan villages across the shining mountains to the great lake, as she called the Pacific ocean."

Patten also told a poignant story of a day when he and Bazil were walking together. They saw an aged Shoshoni woman lying on her back, her shoulders resting on a fifty-pound sack of flour around which a rope was looped. The ends were brought over her shoulders and held in her hands in front.

She was just ready to rise with her burden, and Bazil assisted her to her feet and she trudged off. I told Bazil I thought the load too heavy for such an old person to carry. "See, she is staggering," I said. "Yes, pretty old [replied Bazil]." "She is my mother," and spoke of her connection with Lewis and Clark.

Charles Bocker, a Wyoming pioneer who was driving spikes for the Union Pacific in 1868, wrote that he knew Sacajawea in 1866. He added:

When I was introduced to Sacajawea at Fort Bridger, . . . I should judge at this time she must have been an old woman of about seventy years, . . . quite lovely looking for an old woman, and she could ride horses as well as any of them. . . . I heard at that time when I was at Ft. Bridger, as many

181

times, that she had been with the white men. Everybody all around everywhere knew it, and it was common talk.

This woman, whom many believed to be Sacajawea of the Shoshonis, died on April 9, 1884. Her body was taken from the tipi in which she died and wrapped in skins, which were sewed up for burial. She was placed on her favorite horse, led by Bazil, taken to a coffin, and placed in it. She was buried in the Shoshoni cemetery.

In 1885, the man known on the reservation as Sacajawea's son, Baptiste, died, and was buried by some of the agency Indians in the mountains west of the agency. In the winter of 1886, Bazil, Sacajawea's supposed adopted son, died. Since the ground was frozen, he was placed in a cave on a stream. A leather wallet containing papers, letters, and documents was buried with him. The cave later collapsed and covered the body. In 1924, Andrew, Bazil's son, offered to find the site of his father's grave and gave permission to have the grave opened by Eastman, who was searching for information about the Indian woman. The wallet containing the papers was found, but the papers had disintegrated; Eastman could discern only that there had once been writing on them.

Miss Hebard's first report about Sacajawea was published in the *Journal of American History* in September, 1907, five years after the publication of Mrs. Dye's novel, which had given the Indian girl her first claim to a place in American history. For twenty-five years Miss Hebard continued her efforts to prove that the old Shoshoni woman of the Wind River Reservation was Sacajawea. In 1910 the Bureau of American Ethnology, disregarding Brackenridge's account of meeting Sacajawea in 1811 on the Missouri River, accepted part of Miss Hebard's version of Sacajawea's life.[2] Then, in 1920, John Luttig's journal was published, and readers learned that a wife of Charbonneau's had died at Fort Manuel on December 20, 1812, soon after the birth of a daughter.

It was this publication and the attendant confusion that prompted the commissioner of Indian Affairs to assign Eastman the task of tracing the life of Sacajawea. Eastman made his report in March, 1925. His account largely agreed with Miss Hebard's conclusions, varying only in details. For example, Miss Hebard thought that Bazil was Sacajawea's adopted son; Eastman thought that he was "Toussaint," probably the son of Otter Woman.

Eastman and Miss Hebard had undertaken a nearly impossible task. The Indians had no written language and could only report their recollections orally. By the time the Indian woman's friends and relatives were interviewed, memories were dim. Mrs. James Irwin, wife of the one-time agent on the Wind River Reservation, learned the Shoshoni language, visited with the woman known as Sacajawea, and recorded some of her experiences, including stories she told about the Lewis and Clark Expedition and her later wanderings. Unfortunately a fire at the agency burned Mrs. Irwin's manuscript.

If Sacajawea wandered among the Comanches, as Eastman and Miss Hebard believed, she told them nothing of her experiences or her life with Charbonneau, according to Mr. and Mrs. W. H. Clift, who researched for Miss

[2] Frederick Webb Hodge, "Sacajawea," in *Handbook of American Indians North of Mexico*, II, 401.

Hebard.[3] The Clifts could only report that they encountered "everywhere in some form" the story of a woman who "might have been Sacajawea." The Comanches thought that she had had a Mexican husband at one time and had had at least one child by him. According to Eastman and Miss Hebard, Sacajawea had rejoined her tribe by traveling overland to Fort Bridger with Frémont in 1843. It seems more likely that she would have found her way to western Montana, to ascertain her tribe's whereabouts. Since the United States did not assume authority over the western tribes until 1862, the Shoshonis probably did not move very far east until that date.

The substance of the Shoshoni tradition and the reservation agents' comments was that Porivo was highly respected and that Bazil, the adopted son, was close to his mother, while Baptiste was indifferent to her. (According to those sources, Bazil was more than six feet tall and walked with a limp. Baptiste was short, dark, and uncommunicative.)

Bazil would have had to take his adoptive mother's word for her identity—if he was in truth the boy whom she had adopted when she was with Lewis and Clark. When she rejoined her tribe, Bazil would not have known her, and by then Cameahwait, her brother, was dead.

The Baptiste of this account was only semiliterate and was uncommunicative, preferring ease to activity, and was, in short, altogether different from the gregarious Baptiste whom explorers and fur traders called the best man on foot on the plains or in the Rocky Mountains.

[3] Mrs. Clift was the daughter of William Connelley, at one time secretary of the Kansas Historical Society. She and her husband interviewed many elderly Indians of the Comanche tribe.

The "Sacajawea" of the reservation apparently did not volunteer information, but on occasion she would talk. The sincerity of the people who interviewed her has never been questioned, but they may have been gullible. Any Indian girl who had known Sacajawea in St. Louis, Fort Mandan, or Fort Manuel would have been able to repeat the stories that had been told for years about Sacajawea. French was a common tongue west of the Mississippi, and any Indian who associated with fur traders would speak some French. Charbonneau was known to have had many wives, any one of whom could have claimed to be the wife who went with him to the Pacific Ocean.

The "valuable papers" (the ones buried with Bazil) would have been important evidence in establishing Sacajawea's identity, but unfortunately they proved unreadable.

An Indian woman of later days, Mrs. Esther Burnett Horne, who identified herself as Bazil's great-granddaughter, traveled through the country in the 1950's, speaking earnestly to audiences about her connection with Sacajawea. She was undoubtedly convinced of the truth of the traditional Shoshoni story and wanted to convince others, but she had no further basis for her belief than the foregoing stories.

Eastman, in his report, and Miss Hebard, in her book, elevated Sacajawea to a high position in history—which the Indian girl undoubtedly deserved—but their error lay in trying to reinterpret history. They assumed that Charbonneau came down from the Mandan to St. Louis with two Indian wives and two children. They did not address themselves to the question of why he would do such a thing. He had been invited by Captain Clark to bring one wife and one child, Sacajawea and Baptiste (Pomp). Even if Clark had permitted it, domestic arrangement involving two wives would have been frowned upon in St. Louis.

The record shows that Clark made good his promise to Charbonneau, starting the trapper in farming and, as late as 1820, contributing toward Baptiste's education.

There are two possible explanations for the fact that Sacajawea was not named by either Brackenridge or Bradbury in their journals of 1811. One is that, if only one Shoshoni wife went to St. Louis, then only one could have gone upriver again in 1811 with Charbonneau, and she would have been Sacajawea. Brackenridge, whose identification must carry some weight, said that the woman was the Frenchman's Snake Indian wife and that both she and Charbonneau had accompanied Lewis and Clark. Bradbury confirmed these statements. Sacajawea was generally known as the "Frenchman's squaw" at that time. There were so many fur traders with Indian wives that it did not seem necessary to give the wives first names. The other explanation is that Sacajawea's name was difficult to render in English. Both Lewis and Clark had difficulty pronouncing and spelling it. It was much easier for all concerned to refer to her simply as "Charbonneau's woman."

On December 20, 1812, a year after the boat journey up the Missouri, Luttig reported in his journal the death of the Snake wife of Charbonneau. If Luttig had given Charbonneau's wife a name, a good deal of latter-day speculation and argument would have been avoided. But these contemporary writings, even though incomplete, are persuasive.

It has been argued that Brackenridge's description of Charbonneau's wife failed to match the earlier picture of Sacajawea as an energetic and outgoing girl. He called her "a good creature, of a mild and gentle disposition."[4] It must be remembered that she had lived in St. Louis for five years among white people, whom she wished to emulate, as Brackenridge pointed out—plenty of time for an eager young woman to learn the "rules" of white women's deportment.

It has been questioned, too, whether Sacajawea could be called "sickly," as she was by Brackenridge, in view of the endurance she displayed on the long journey with Lewis and Clark. Such arguments again fail to consider the intervening years, in which Sacajawea matured from girlhood to womanhood—and in an unfamiliar environment, a frontier settlement, where she may easily have become victim to the many ills of so-called civilization. Indeed, the "fever" that Luttig reports as the cause of Sacajawea's death at Fort Manuel may very well have been caused by an infection to which the Indian girl (as well as another Shoshoni woman at Fort Manuel, the wife of Josef Elie) had no resistance. There is also the possibility that complications following the birth of the daughter, Lizette, caused her death.

No burial site has been discovered in the region of Fort Manuel, although it is known that several persons died there. The two Shoshoni wives no doubt received a burial

4 Neta Lohnes Frazier has suggested that Brackenridge's description did not fit Sacajawea, who "so irritates her husband that he beats her," who "berates Clark when he displeases her," and who "demands her rights to go to the ocean to see the whale" (*Sacajawea: The Girl Nobody Knows*, 140). What we know of Sacajawea from the journals indicates that she was anything but irritating, quarrelsome, and demanding. Nor do we know that Charbonneau was a wife beater or that Sacajawea ever displeased Clark or that she "demanded her rights."

in the ground, after the manner of the white people, but excavations made around the site of the fort, which was abandoned and burned nearly one hundred and fifty years ago, have not revealed any human skeletons. Sacajawea may have been buried on one of the hills not far from the fort. However, with Sioux war parties so close in December, 1812, it would seem more likely that the burial place was near the stockade, though an armed party could have been sent to oversee interment in a more suitable area.

In 1883 the Reverend John Roberts, mentioned earlier, became missionary at the Shoshoni reservation in Wyoming and remained there for forty-nine years. In 1884 he officiated at the funeral of the woman he later identified as "Sacajawea of the Shoshonis." But he could have had only slight acquaintance with her. Moreover, at the time of her death he evidently did not know that she was reputed to be the Sacajawea of the famous expedition. The official form he completed at the time of her death states only that she was "Bazil's mother." Only later did Mr. Roberts comment on her supposed identity: "I read over her grave the burial services of the Episcopal church. I little realized that the heroine we laid to rest, in years to come would become one of the outstanding women of American history."

At the time of the woman's funeral a small wooden slab was placed at the head of her grave; later, boulders were set at the head and foot. A stone marker was erected there in 1909 by H. E. Wadsworth, the Shoshoni agent. The marker was the gift of Timothy F. Burke, of Cheyenne, Wyoming.

It appears certain that an estimable Shoshoni woman lies buried on the Wind River Reservation, with a son on each side of her. It is equally certain, however, no written evidence or surviving objects prove that she was Sacajawea of the Lewis and Clark Expedition.

In 1955 a notebook belonging to Clark was discovered.[5] The book was apparently used by Clark between 1825 and 1828. On the outside of the book, in his writing, appears a list of names of members of the expedition, with notations about what happened to each one after the journey or his residence at the time the notes were made. Beside Sacajawea's name, which Clark spelled "Secarjaweau," he wrote one word: "Dead."

He also listed Lewis, Odoway (Ordway), Floyd, Gass, Collins, Colter, J. Fields, Goodrich, McNeal, Shields, and LePage as "dead." He listed Cruzatte, Potts, Wiser, and Drewyer as "killed." Some others he named with a possible place of residence (as, "N. Pryor at Fort Smith; R. Fields near Louisville"); and some he named without further notations. He included others who were not members of the permanent party which left from the Mandan villages. He also wrote "Tous. Charbono Mand" (Mandans?), "Tousant Charbon in Wertenburgh, Gy." (by "Tousant Charbon" Clark unquestionably meant Baptiste). This notation dates the document between 1824 and 1829, since those are the years Baptiste was known to have been with Prince Paul in Württtemberg.

Clark was wrong about one member of the expedition, Gass, whom he reported dead. Patrick Gass lived to be almost one hundred years old. In 1962, Donald Jackson wrote:

We are hardly justified in saying "If Clark was wrong about

[5] Now in the Newberry Library, Chicago.

Gass, then perhaps he is wrong about Sacagawea," for the cases are different. Gass had gone back to Virginia and severed his contacts with the West, but Sacagawea, her husband, Charbonneau, and her children were Clark's concern for many years after the expedition. He cared about them and felt a kind of responsibility for them. It is difficult to believe he could have been wrong about Sacagawea's death.[6]

In 1956, Will G. Robinson, secretary for the South Dakota State Historical Society, wrote: "It seems most improbable that she was buried at any other place [than Fort Manuel].... We think that the entry in the Clark Journal writes 'finis' to the controversy." He added:

I, for one, am much better pleased with a feeling that this truly great woman died at Ft. Manuel ... rather than try to follow the vague and nebulous wanderings of a woman who had many husbands, followed the hard life of a drudge among the fur traders and died wholly unrecognized.[7]

Certainly this seems a reasonable conclusion. The traditional account of her quarrel with Charbonneau and her subsequent wanderings is vague and unsupported by written record. And yet, as Jack R. Gage has pointed out, even written records can be fallible. The journals of explorers

[6] Donald Jackson (ed.), *Letters of the Lewis and Clark Expedition*, 639.

[7] Many Indian women were reduced to drudges. Often they were substitutes for pack animals. At Fort Mandan Lewis and Clark reported that She-he-ke brought to the fort a quarter of beef on his wife's back. On another occasion a woman carried a canoe three miles on her back. When Clark's "whale party" was returning from Tillamook Head, he tried to help a Chinook woman whose load of blubber had slipped, but he found the load so heavy that he could barely lift it. Finally her husband came back to help her.

and mountain men have their share of errors.[8] All that the serious researcher can do is to judge, on the basis of verifiable fact and reliable documentation, what he believes to be the truth.

In this context, still another version of Sacajawea's death must be considered. In 1947, John Bakeless reported that a Hidatsa warrior, Bull's Eye, speaking in open council, where other Indians could hear (and correct) his story, claimed to be the grandson of Sacajawea, wife of "Sharbonish," with whom she went "far away somewhere." She was killed, Bull's Eye said, by hostile Indians near Glasgow, Montana, in 1869, when he himself was four years old.[9] This version of Sacajawea's death has never been authenticated.

In sum, documentary evidence seems to indicate clearly that Sacajawea died at Fort Manuel, South Dakota, in 1812 and lies buried there in some unmarked grave. The independent records of Brackenridge, Bradbury, Luttig, and later of Clark seem to permit no other reasonable conclusion. And yet, despite the evidence, there will always be those who prefer to believe that Sacajawea, the heroine of the Lewis and Clark Expedition, lived to be nearly one hundred years old and died venerated by her tribe on the Wind River Reservation in Wyoming. Each year many persons visit the reservation to see the stone erected in her memory in 1963 by the Wyoming State Organization of the National Society of Daughters of the American Revolution. The marker reads: "Sacajawea, Died April 9, 1884. A Guide with the Lewis and Clark Expedition, 1805–1806.

[8] Jack R. Gage, *Wyoming Afoot and Horseback: History Mostly Ain't True.*

[9] Bakeless, *Lewis and Clark,* 455.

Identified, 1907, by Rev. J. Roberts, Who Officiated at Her Burial."

It may never be known for certain whether Sacajawea lived a short life or a long one—whether she died in her twenties at a white men's fort in South Dakota or at an old age on a reservation in Wyoming. In a sense her chapter in history ended in 1806, with the successful conclusion of the Lewis and Clark Expedition. Perhaps the most enduring picture that can be conjured up of this remarkable woman is of an Indian girl bearing a baby on her back, gathering berries along a riverbank for a boatload of explorers bound on America's great westward adventure.

SACAJAWEA, *by Charles M. Russell*
COURTESY OF NATIONAL COWBOY HALL OF FAME AND WESTERN
HERITAGE CENTER, OKLAHOMA CITY

Appendices

River

Sacajawea Creek, Montana, named by Lewis and Clark. It
flows into the Missouri River near the confluence of the
Musselshell (now known as Crooked Creek).

Statues

Louisiana Purchase Exposition Grounds, St. Louis, Bruno Louis Zimm, 1904.

Lakeview Terrace, now in City Park, Portland, Oregon, Alice Cooper, 1905.

Indian girl pointing the way for Lewis and Clark, Cyrus Edwin Dallin, 1910.

Bronze statue, erected by Federation of Women's Clubs and school children of North Dakota, Capitol Building grounds, Bismarck, North Dakota, Leonard Crunelle, 1910.

Group, Lewis and Clark and Indian girl, Public Square, Charlottesville, Virginia.

Group, Sacajawea with Lewis and Clark, Charles M. Russell, National Cowboy Hall of Fame and Western Heritage Center, Oklahoma City.

Mountains

Sacajawea Peak, Bridger Range, Montana.

Sacagawea Peak, Wind River Range, Wyoming.

Sacajawea Peak, Wallowa Range, Oregon.

Sacajawea Peak, Lost River Range, Idaho.

Paintings

Sacajawea on Indian pony, with child in papoose cradle, Henry Altman, 1905.

Sacajawea, State University of Montana Library, Edward Samuel Paxson, 1906.

Mural, *Lewis and Clark at Three Forks*, Edward Samuel Paxson, Capitol, Helena, Montana.

The Shoshonis Naming Sacajawea, Tullius P. Dunlap, 1925.

Mural, Capitol, Helena, Montana, representing meeting of Sacajawea and her brother, Charles M. Russell, 1912.

Painting, Sacajawea in boat meeting Chinook party, Amon Carter Museum of Western Art, Fort Worth, Texas, Charles M. Russell.

Markers

Grave of "Sacajawea of the Shoshonis," on the Shoshoni Reservation, near Lander, Wyoming, 1909.

Sacajawea marker, near Tendoy, Idaho, west of Lemhi Pass.

Bronze tablet on wall of Bishop Randall Chapel, Shoshoni Cemetery, Wyoming, 1931.

Granite marker, Shoshoni Cemetery, for Bazil, Baptiste, and Baptiste's daughter Barbara Meyers, 1932.

Boulder with bronze tablet, honoring meeting place of Sacajawea and her brother, Cameahwait, near the confluence of Horse Prairie and Red Rock creeks, Armstead, Montana, 1914.

Boulder and brass tablet erected by Daughters of American Revolution, near Three Forks, Montana, 1914.

Monument near Mobridge, South Dakota, 1929.

Lakes

Lake Sacajawea, Longview, Washington.

Lake Sakakawea (formerly Lake Garrison), North Dakota.

Music

"Sacajawea," intermezzo, Rollin Bond, bandmaster, New York City, 1904.

"Sacajawea," song, lyrics by Porter Bryan Coolidge, of Lander, Wyoming, music by Frederick Bouthroyd, Leicester, England, 1924.

"The Bird Woman, Sacajawea: A Legend of the Trail of the West," cantata, Toledo Choral Society, text by Evangeline Close, music by William Lester, 1932.

Miscellaneous

Silver service set, battleship *Wyoming*, 1912. Now at University of Wyoming.

Pageant, 1915, Beaverhead River valley.

Sacajawea Museum, Spalding, Idaho (destroyed by floods, 1964; see Appendix B).

Airplane, *Spirit of Sacajawea*, first flight, July, 1927, over Shoshoni National Forest, Wyoming.

Sacajawea State Park, near Pasco and Kennewick, Washington, including wooden marker and carved inscription.

Pageant, 1955, Three Forks, Montana.

Sacajawea Springs, south fork of Payette River, Idaho.

Camp Sacajawea for Girl Scouts, Casper Mountain, Casper, Wyoming.

Bronze casting of model by Henry Lion from sketch by Charles M. Russell for monument showing Sacajawea pointing the way for Lewis and Clark, Montana Historical Society Museum, Helena, Montana, 1958.

B. THE LAND OF THE NEZ PERCÉS

The area around Spalding, Idaho, is Nez Percé country. There Lewis and Clark first encountered Indians of that tribe. Today the area east of Spalding is the Nez Percé Reservation. The town was named for the Reverend Henry Spalding, who built his second mission, then called Lapwai, there in 1838.

Canoe Camp, at which Lewis and Clark built dugout canoes in the autumn of 1805 and cached supplies and from which they set off down the Clearwater, is about five miles west of Orofino in Canoe Camp State Park, on U.S. 12. Weippe Prairie is about eight miles southwest of Grangeville on U.S. 95. It was once covered with grass and the blue-flowered camas. About a mile and a half north of the highway bridge at Kamiah, on U.S. 12, Lewis and Clark camped for the better part of a month in the spring of 1806, on their way home.

The Sacajawea Museum, once located at Spalding, was destroyed by flood in 1964. It contained equipment, including a canoe, said to have been used by members of the expedition. A Nez Percé National Historical Park in this region has been authorized by Congress but has not yet been established.

Bibliography

Alter, J. Cecil. *James Bridger*. Salt Lake City, 1925.

American State Papers, 1820. Missouri Historical Society, St. Louis.

Anderson, Irving W. "J. B. Charbonneau, Son of Sacajawea," *Oregon Historical Quarterly*, Vol. LXXI, No. 3 September, 1970).

Andrews, Wayne, ed. *The Concise Dictionary of American History*. New York, 1962.

Andrist, Ralph K. *To the Pacific with Lewis and Clark*. New York, 1967.

Bakeless, John. *The Journals of Lewis and Clark*. New York, 1964.

———. *Lewis and Clark: Partners in Discovery*. New York, 1947.

Bleeker, Sonia. *Indians*. New York, 1963.

Boggs, W. M. "Manuscript on Bent's Fort, 1844–1845," ed. by LeRoy R. Hafen, *Colorado Magazine*, Vol. VII, No. 2 (March, 1930).

Botkin, B. A. *Western Folklore*. New York, 1962.

Brackenridge, Henry M. *Journal of a Voyage up the Missouri River in 1811*. Pittsburgh, 1814. (Also in Thwaites, *Early Western Travels, q.v.*)

Bradbury, John. *Travels in the Interior of America in the Years 1809, 1810 and 1811*. London, 1819. (Also in Thwaites, *Early Western Travels, q.v.*)

Brown, James S. *Life of a Pioneer*. Salt Lake City, 1900.

Burnet, John C. Letters, manuscripts, photographs, and interviews. Hebard Collection, University of Wyoming, Laramie.

Burnett, F. G. Letters, manuscripts, and typed interviews. Hebard Collection, University of Wyoming, Laramie.

Campbell, Walter S. *Kit Carson*. New York, 1928.

Catlin, George. *Manners, Customs and Conditions of the North American Indians*. 2 vols. London, 1841.

Chandler, Katherine. *Bird Woman of the Lewis and Clark Expedition*. New York, 1905.

Chardon, Francis A. Fort Clark Journals. Ed. by Annie Heloise Abel. Pierre, S.Dak., 1932.

Chittenden, Hiram M. *The American Fur Trade of the Far West.* 3 vols. New York, 1902.

Clark, W. P. *Indian Sign Language.* Philadelphia, 1885.

Clarke, Charles G. *The Men of the Lewis and Clark Expedition.* Glendale, Calif., 1970.

Clift, Edith Connelley. Manuscripts. Hebard Collection, University of Wyoming, Laramie.

Clift, W. H. Manuscripts. University of Wyoming, Laramie.

Coues, Elliott. *A History of the Expedition Under the Command of Captains Lewis and Clark.* 3 vols. New York, 1965. (First published in 4 vols., 1893.)

Crawford, Helen. "Sakakawea," *North Dakota Historical Quarterly,* Vol. I, No. 3 (April, 1927).

Defenbach, B. *Red Heroines of the Northwest.* Caldwell, 1929.

De Voto, Bernard, ed. *The Journals of Lewis and Clark.* Boston, 1963.

Dye, Eva Emery. *The Conquest.* Chicago, 1902.

Eastman, Charles A. Original letters, 1925. Hebard Collection, University of Wyoming, Laramie.

Eidie, Ingvard Henry. *American Odyssey: The Journal of Lewis and Clark.* Chicago, 1969.

El Hult, Ruby. *Guns of the Lewis and Clark Expedition.* Washington State Historical Society, Tacoma.

Emory, W. H. *Notes on Cooke, Johnson, Abert. Ft. Leavenworth in Missouri to San Diego in California, 1840–1847.* Washington, D.C., 1848.

Ferris, W. A. "Life in the Rocky Mountains, 1830–1835," *Western Literary Messenger*, in *Wonderland*, 1901.

Frazier, Neta Lohnes. *Sacajawea: The Girl Nobody Knows.* New York, 1967.

Frémont, John C. *Report of the Exploring Expedition to the Rocky Mountains.* Washington, D.C., 1845.

Fuller, George W. *History of the Pacific Northwest.* New York, 1931.

Gage, Jack R. *Wyoming Afoot and Horseback: History Mostly Ain't True.* Cheyenne, 1966.

Gass, Patrick. *Journal of the Lewis and Clark Expedition.* Philadelphia, 1810; Chicago, 1904.

Ghent, W. J. *The Early Far West.* New York, 1936.

The Great West. New York, 1965.

Grinnell, George Bird. *Blackfoot Lodge Tales.* Lincoln, 1962.

Hafen, Ann W. "Baptiste Charbonneau, Son of Bird Woman," in *The Mountain Men and the Fur Trade of the Far West*, Vol. I. Glendale, 1965.

Hebard, Grace Raymond. *Sacajawea: Guide of the Lewis and Clark Expedition.* Los Angeles, 1957 (first published in 1932).

Henry, Alexander, and David Thompson. *Manuscript Journals, 1799–1814.* Ed. by Elliott Coues. 3 vols. New York, 1897.

Hodge, Frederick Webb. "Sacajawea," in *Handbook of American Indians North of Mexico*, Vol. II. Washington, D.C., 1910.

Hosmer, James K. *History of the Louisiana Purchase.* New York, 1902.

Hunt, Theodore. Minutes. Testimony Relating to Lands in

the Towns and Villages of St. Louis, Etc., Feb. 13 to May 25, 1825. Missouri Historical Society, St. Louis.

Indians. New York, 1961.

Indians of the Americas. Washington, D.C., 1967.

Indians of the Plains. New York, 1967.

Jackson, Donald, ed. *Letters of the Lewis and Clark Expedition.* Urbana, 1963.

Karsten, M. O. *Hunter and Interpreter for Lewis and Clark, George Drouillard.* Glendale, 1968.

Kennerly, William Clark. "Hunting Buffaloes in the Early Forties." Missouri Historical Society, St. Louis.

Kingston, C. S. "Sacajawea as Guide," *Pacific Northwest Quarterly*, Vol. XXXV (January, 1944).

Larpenteur, Charles. *Forty Years a Fur Trader on the Upper Missouri.* Ed. by Elliott Coues. 2 vols. New York, 1898.

Lewis, Meriwether. *The Lewis and Clark Expedition.* Ed. by Nicholas Biddle. 3 vols. Philadelphia, 1961 (originally published in 1814).

———, and William Clark. *Original Journals of the Lewis and Clark Expedition, 1804–1806.* Ed. by Reuben Gold Thwaites. 8 vols. New York, 1904.

Lisa, Manuel. Collection of letters, 1794–1820. Missouri Historical Society, St. Louis.

Lowie, Robert H. *Indians of the Plains.* New York, 1954.

Luttig, John C. *Journal of a Fur Trading Expedition on the Upper Missouri, 1812–1813.* Ed. by Stella M. Drumm. New York, 1964 (first published by the Missouri Historical Society, St. Louis, in 1920).

McCracken, Harold. *George Catlin and the Old Frontier.* New York, 1959.

Maximilian, Prince of Wied. *Travels in the Interior of North America*. London, 1843.

Meek, Joseph. *River of the West*. Ed. by Frances Fuller Victor. Hartford, Conn., 1870.

Mencken, Henry L. *The American Language*. 4th ed. New York, 1960.

Morison, Samuel Eliot. *The Oxford History of the American People*. New York, 1968.

O'Meara, Walter. *Daughters of the Country*. New York, 1968.

Ordway, John. Journal. Wisconsin State Historical Society, Madison.

Patten, James I. Letters and manuscripts. Hebard Collection, University of Wyoming, Laramie.

Poole, Edwin A. "Charbono's Squar," *Pacific Northwesterner*, Vol. VIII, No. 3.

Porter, Clyde H. "Jean Baptiste Charbonneau," *Idaho Yesterdays*, Vol. V, No. 3.

Quaife, M. M. *Journals of Captain Meriwether Lewis and Sergeant John Ordway*, Madison, 1916.

Rees, John E. "The Shoshoni Contribution to Lewis and Clark," *Idaho Yesterdays*, Vol. II, No. 2.

Rivington, Tom. Original letters and manuscripts. Hebard Collection, University of Wyoming, Laramie.

Roberts, John. Letters and manuscripts. Hebard Collection, University of Wyoming, Laramie.

Robinson, Doane. *Brief History of South Dakota*. New York, 1919.

———. "Sacajawea vs. Sakakawea" (address before the

Academy of Science and Letters), Sioux City, Iowa, January 24, 1924.

Ruxton, George Frederick. *Adventures in Mexico and in the Rocky Mountains*. New York, 1848.

———. *Life in the Far West*. Norman, 1951.

Salisbury, Albert, and Jane Salisbury. *Two Captains West*. New York, 1950.

Schultz, J. W. *The Bird Woman: Guide of Lewis and Clark*. Boston, 1918.

Scott, L. T. *Sacajawea: The Unsung Heroine of Montana*. Armstead, 1915.

Siebert, Jerry. *Sacajawea*. Boston, 1960.

Smith, E. Willard. "Journal While with the Fur Traders, Vásquez and Sublette in the Rocky Mountain Region," *Oregon Historical Society Quarterly*, Vol. XIV, No. 3 (September, 1913).

Snyder, Gerald S. *In the Footsteps of Lewis and Clark*. Washington, D.C., 1970.

Speck, Gordon. *Breeds and Half-Breeds*. New York, 1969.

Thwaites, Reuben Gold, ed. *Early Western Travels, 1748–1846*. 32 vols. Cleveland, 1904–1906.

———. *Original Journals of the Lewis and Clark Expedition, 1804–1806*. New York, 1904.

Tomkins, Calvin. *The Lewis and Clark Trail*. New York, 1965.

U.S. Superintendent of Indian Affairs. *Correspondence of William Clark and Others at St. Louis, 1813–1855*. 29 vols. Kansas State Historical Society, Topeka.

Vestal, Stanley (pseud. of Walter S. Campbell). *The Missouri*. New York, 1945.

Wheeler, O. D. *The Trail of Lewis and Clark, 1804–1806.* 2 vols. Hartford, 1870.

Whitehouse, Joseph, ed. *Journal of the Lewis and Clark Expedition, 1804–1806.* New York, 1904. (Also in Thwaites, *Early Western Travels, q.v.*)

Wyoming State Journal, December 3, 1930.

Index